Yesterday's Adventure

McKenzie Pass, ca. 1927.

YESTERDAY'S ADVENTURE

A Photographic History of
Lane County, Oregon

**LANE COUNTY
HISTORICAL SOCIETY**

EUGENE, OREGON
1998

Yesterday's Adventure
A Photographic History of Lane County, Oregon

A publication of the
Lane County Historical Society
PO Box 11532
Eugene, Oregon 97440

Photos from Lane County Historical Museum, unless otherwise credited

Publications committee
Ken Metzler, Editor
Lucile McKenzie
Barbara Huntington Pitney
Donald T. Smith

Copyright © 1998 by Lane County Historical Society
ISBN 0-9648434-2-0 (hardcover edition)
ISBN 0-9648434-1-2 (paperback edition)

Yesterday's Adventure
A Photographic History of Lane County, Oregon
Series: Lane County Histories, No. 1

Cover Photo: Slicing through snow the height of car tops, a caravan winds its way across the McKenzie Pass in the Cascade Mountains of eastern Lane County, a circa 1927 scene. (Photo: Chester Stevenson.)

Contents

Preface/Acknowledgments

THIS PROJECT by the Lane County Historical Society derives from a certain lusty curiosity about the content of the photographic files of the Lane County Historical Museum, not to mention the archives of other museums, the Willamette National Forest, and private collections. The society's four-member book committee selected what we considered the best photographs to depict early life in such a dramatically diverse land as Lane County. As we scanned countless photos, sometimes a simple exclamation by one of our members—"Oh, wow!"—was enough endorsement to include the photo in our selection.

We owe a debt of gratitude to many people, not least of which are the photographers, professional and amateur, whose works found their way into the archives and thus onto these pages. Thanks belong also to the men and women who, down through the years, took the trouble to set forth their experiences and observations on paper, or who in later years submitted to taped interviews. How else would we know some of the vignettes that depict life in the early days—such things as kids in Lorane roaming the virgin forested hills by themselves ("I don't know why we kids didn't get lost ....") or the "women problems" of a lonely bachelor or the "men problems" of the single ladies in Deadwood Valley. We've detailed some of these experiences in written comments that supplement the photos.

We have tried to be diligent in preparing a bibliography that recognizes the sources consulted in the preparation of this book. Standing out among them is the late Hallie Hills Huntington who seemed to recognize from the beginning that, as granddaughter of wagon train immigrant Cornelius Hills, her historical observations would be an invaluable written record of life in the early years of this century.

Thanks also to Ed Stelfox, Lane County Historical Museum; Louis Campbell, Siuslaw Pioneer Museum, Florence; Margaret Leaming, Oakridge Pioneer Museum; Carol Winkler, Willamette National Forest; Cindy Heidemann, University of Oregon Bookstore; Cliff Minks, lab technician at Dotson's Photo Shop. Also Misty Post, Curtis Irish, Ron Byers, Steve McQuiddy, Bill Loy, Jerold Williams, Claudia Miller, John McWade, Robert Cox, Ethan L. Newman, Janet K. Burg, Marjory Smith, Betty Metzler, Eric Gustafson, Gwen Rhoads.

Special thanks to A. J. (Jim) Giustina, president of the Lane County Historical Society, for the help and encouragement.

No one named above is responsible for any errors that may have crept unannounced into this book: please blame the undersigned, members of the Historical Society's publication committee.

KEN METZLER, EDITOR
LUCILE MCKENZIE
BARBARA HUNTINGTON PITNEY
DONALD T. SMITH

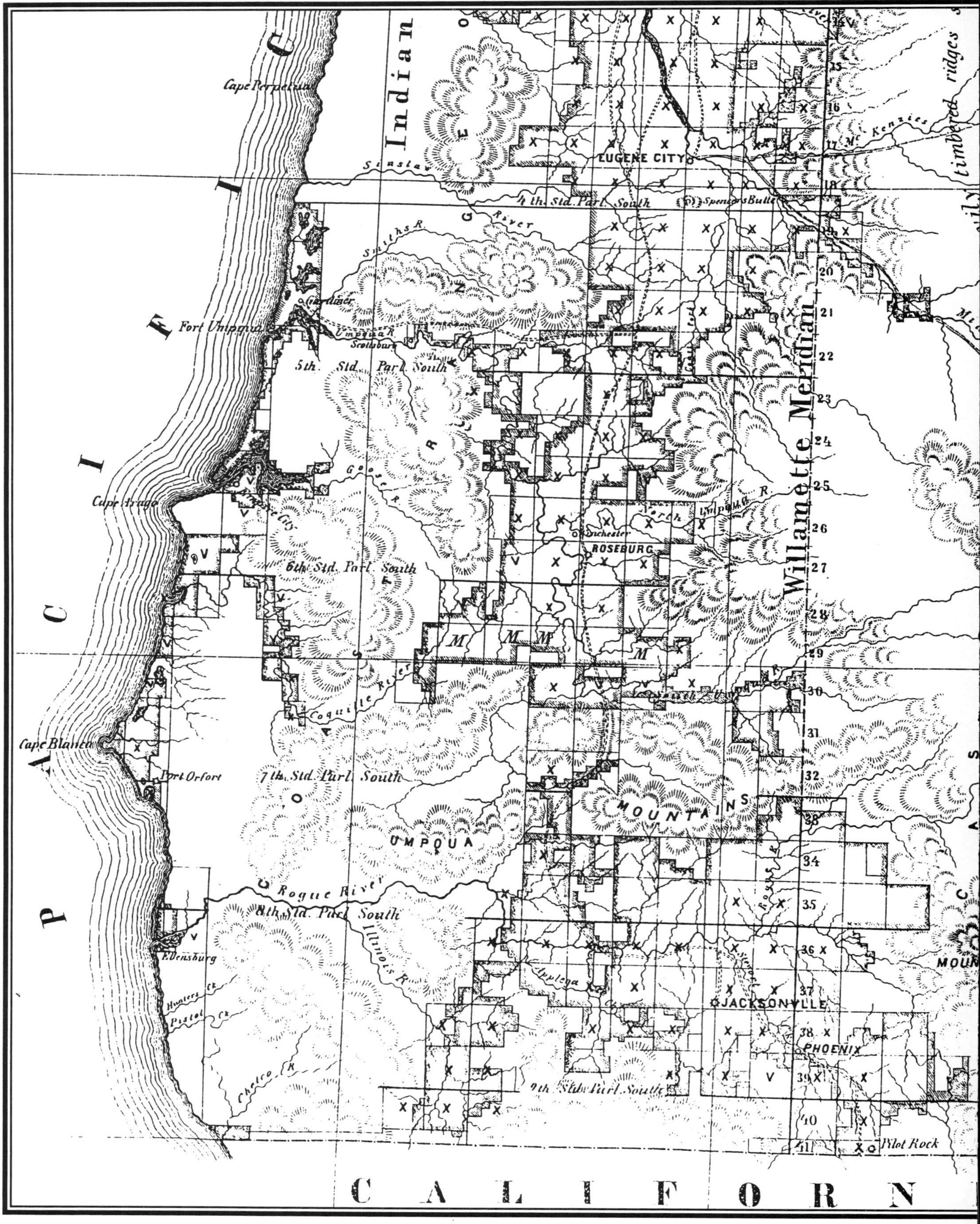
P A C I F I C
Indian
Cape Perpetua
EUGENE CITY
4th. Std. Parl. South
Spencers Butte
Smiths R.
Gardiner
Fort Umpqua
Umpqua R.
Scottsburg
5th. Std. Parl. South
Willamette Meridian
Cape Arago
Goose R.
ROSEBURG
6th Std. Parl. South
Coquille River
Cape Blanco
Port Orford
7th Std. Parl. South
MOUNTAINS
UMPQUA
Rogue River
8th Std. Parl. South
Illinois R.
Ellensburg
Hunters Ck
Pistol Ck
Chetco R.
JACKSONVILLE
PHOENIX
9th Std. Parl. South
Pilot Rock
timbered ridges
C A L I F O R N

CHAPTER ONE

Mysterious Country

THE MAP ON THE OPPOSITE PAGE suggests just how mysterious was the country we've come to revere as Lane County. We now know it as the site of a most pleasant and awesome variety of rivers, lakes, coastal beaches and dunes, fertile valleys, forested ranges, and glacier-clad mountains. But as late as 1863, the date of this map prepared by the Surveyor General's Office in Eugene City, the mountain areas north and south of the Siuslaw River were a mystery. There's no hint of Oregon's largest coast range lake, Triangle Lake, for example. And in the Cascade Mountains to the east, take note of two lakes south of the Three Sisters Peaks and northeast of Diamond Peak: "Virgin Lakes." You will not find even one Virgin Lake there on any map today or any other lake shaped as this map shows. The area had not been surveyed, and the map makers apparently sketched in a couple of lakes on the basis of reported sightings, perhaps of the ones we now call Waldo and Odell lakes.

Exploring Lane County thus became an adventure throughout its history, and it continues to be an adventure to this day.

Eventually the scenic treasures of Lane County's far reaches became surveyed, plotted with precision on maps, and known to all. Meanwhile settlers moved in, communities such as Skinner's (later Eugene City) and Pleasant Hill developed. Especially adventurous settlers probed ever deeper into the nether reaches to places like Deadwood and McKenzie Bridge.

In the later stages of these explorations and developments, photographers began to record the process. Their work, depicted on the succeeding pages, will allow you to share in the sense of discovery—to see this varied land as it revealed itself little by little to early residents—and perhaps even to see Lane County as a grand adventure still in the making.◆

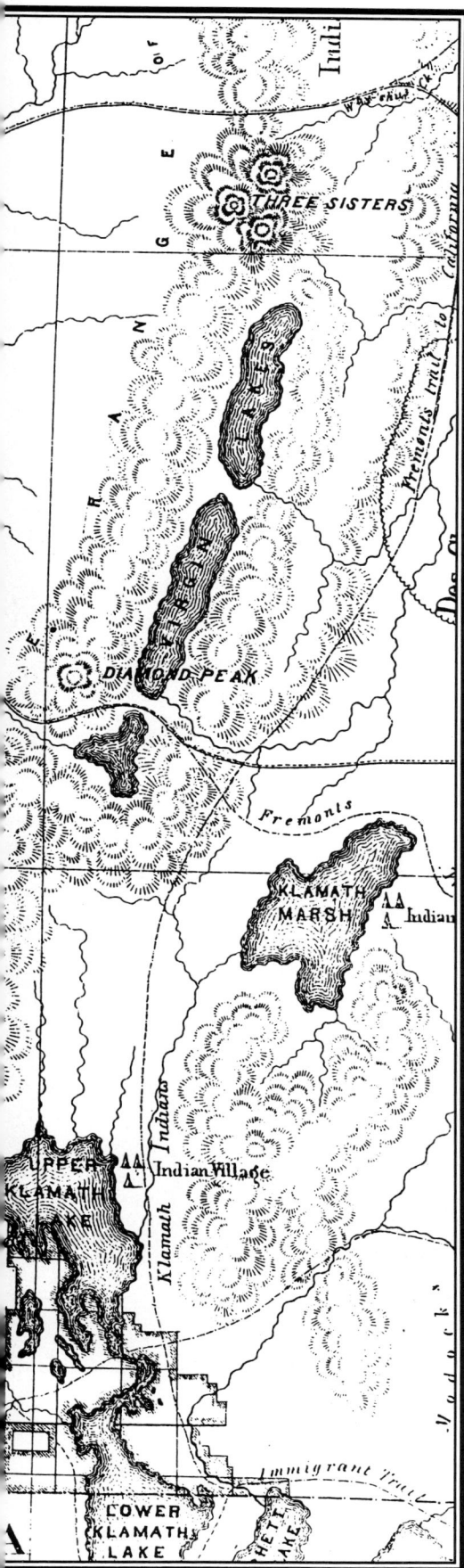

Mariners were the first Europeans to view the pristine land of "New Albion," a name attached to the Pacific Northwest by Sir Francis Drake in 1579. Spanish mariner Bruno de Heceta sailed past here in 1775 and gave his name to the headland in the background: Heceta Head. This 1892 photo predates the famous Heceta Lighthouse by two years. This beach scene eventually became Devil's Elbow State Park.

CHAPTER TWO

Pristine Country

IMAGINE TREKKING 125 MILES from the Oregon Coast to the mountains along the 44th parallel of north latitude. You'll traverse headlands and peaks, valleys and forested river canyons. Translate the ups and downs into musical notes, and you have a symphony in four movements. It starts here at the coast, perhaps a blustery drum rattle to represent the smashing seas in winter. Then a scherzo or two to trip lightly over the Coast Range. Next a slower third movement, a pastorale, to bring us across the valley of the Willamette River. Finally a vibrant build of tempo crossing the Cascade Mountains, up the slopes with kettle drums thundering and cymbals clanging until we reach the tops of three snowy, wind-swept 10,000-foot peaks, the Three Sisters.

That's Lane County then and now. The topography has not changed much in 175 years since botanist David Douglas explored this land in November 1826. Nor has the weather. So fierce was the rain and wind on that trip that Douglas' party couldn't start a fire while camped west of present-day Eugene. "All hungry and no means of cooking," he wrote. "Drenched and bleached with rain and sleet, chilled with a piercing north wind; and then to finish the day, experiencing the cooling, comfortless consolation of lying down without supper or fire. On such occasions I am liable to become fretful." (Beckham, p. 231.)

Water, sometimes too much of it, remains the essence of this region. Multiply the "average" precipitation of Lane County (46.04" says *Oregon Blue Book*) by the size of Lane County. You get a figure that suggests more water falls here than on any of Oregon's other 35 counties. A simplistic calculation, no doubt. But it would not have surprised David Douglas, for whom the Douglas fir is named, a tree destined to become a mainstay of the economy.

Water—as rain, snow, lakes, rivers, and giant floods—sculpts and refines the rough draft of volcanic geology. It helps to clothe this raw terrain with soft mantles of vast green forests and grasses that delight the eye and power the economy. Water, in short, has helped to grow turnips and trees and to form delightful valleys and knolls.

Pioneer immigrant Elijah Bristow visited this country in 1846, arriving at rolling terrain southeast of Eugene. "What a pleasant hill!" he exclaimed. "It reminds me of my childhood home in Virginia. I will settle here."

And he did, building his home in a region called Pleasant Hill ever since. He and other settlers knew little of the astonishing variety of scenic delights that awaited them, so concerned were they with scratching out a living on the land. Eventually they flourished. They and others to follow began to explore the delights of a pristine country represented by these photos.

The eastern end of what was to become Lane County, appears as mysterious and foreboding as the coast. Early settlers did not have mountains in mind except as barriers blocking easy access to the rich farmlands of the Willamette Valley. Eventually, though, such mountain wilderness scenes would appeal to latter-day Oregon Trail trekkers arriving in increasing numbers, backpacks and instant food mixes at the ready. This view shows Three Sisters peaks about 1960. (Photo: Deland Aerial, Willamette National Forest.)

Around every bend awaiting discovery by pioneer residents were sites of incredible scenic splendor such as this 286-foot waterfall, second highest in Oregon: Salt Creek Falls, shown here encrusted in ice and fringed by icicles.
(Photo: L. Parker, Willamette National Forest, 1964.)

Discovered at last—the 6,000-acre mystery, once called
Virgin Lake, then Pengra Lake, now known as Waldo Lake,
named for John B. Waldo of Salem, a judge and Cascade
Mountain adventurer. (Photo: Willamette National Forest.)

Upper McKenzie River delight. About 1874 Rollin Belknap
(founder of Belknap Hot Springs Resort) and Thomas M.
Martin (minister and postmaster at Vida) hiked 20 miles
upstream from Belknap Resort past these falls to Clear
Lake, source of the McKenzie. They were the first white men
of record to view the lake. The pair crossed the river at the
top of the falls via long fir poles they had cut and laid across.
Belknap boldly walked upright across the wiggly poles,
seemingly oblivious to the danger. Martin, for whom the
river's famous Martin Rapids are named, got down on hands
and knees and "cooned it" across. (Inman, p. 115.) Sahalie
Falls belongs to neighboring Linn County, but Lane County's
McKenzie River folks claim a proxy ownership.
(Photo: Schillios Photography, 1955.)

A fur trapper and explorer named Donald McKenzie discovered this cold, clear stream in 1812. "Picture the river as it must have been in those days," suggested early river guide Prince Helfrich, "a clear, cold river untouched by man, and teeming with trout and salmon. Birds and game were plentiful. Many deer and elk browsed along the shores, and an occasional Indian trod the paths which closely followed the river." (Helfrich, p. 15.)

For all its extreme reaches from the sea to the mountains, Lane County is probably best known historically for its meandering Willamette River and the fertile agricultural valley that surrounds it. This pastoral scene was near Eugene about 1908.

Water helps to define Lane County, but. . . . Initially the Willamette flowed free, and its frequent floods enriched the agricultural lands in the valley with deposits of river loam. But the river's free-wheeling excesses became a problem when people dared to erect structures in its flood path, as here about 1925.

CHAPTER THREE

Making a Home

Carving a home out of the wilderness: Zilphia and Stephen Rigdon at Rigdon Meadow east of Oakridge in 1890. With them are children left in their care. Thirty-seven years earlier, the "Lost Wagon Train of 1853" awaited rescue at Pine Opening, near this site. Some 300 wagon train settlers had taken a "shortcut," deviating from the original Oregon Trail to a southern route across eastern and central Oregon. They arrived here in the Cascade Mountains late in the season, tired, starving, and discouraged. A rescue party brought them food and supplies.

"HOME IS THE BEST PLACE AFTER ALL," declared Zilphia Bristow Rigdon in her diary after returning from camping. Much as she loved to explore the mountains, she loved home more.

In 1856 Zilphia started a diary of home life—"to write whatsoever nonsense I wish to fill it up with." She recorded almost every meal: "Our first meal at home was dinner; cabbage greens, meat, & gravy, biscuits & milk."

Her husband, Stephen Rigdon, established a high-mountain trading post east of Oakridge. The rustic cabin shown here was Zilphia's summer home. Her diary cites both routine and high points of country life.

"I will have to quit and go milk the cows before it gets dark."

"At the state fair in 1866 took a first-premium quilt (3 dollars)." (Keepers.)

Home life varied widely in a county so diverse. For some loggers and miners, home was a bunkhouse in the remote woods. Children of married couples attended school in boxcars parked on sidings. Shopping meant long rail trips out of the woods. Bachelors suffered loneliness. At the remote, often snow-bound Bohemia mines east of Cottage Grove, an "old engineer" contacted a matrimonial bureau and secured names of six prospects. "He is getting old & a little bit childish," a fellow miner wrote. "He wants to be sure that 'them widders' are not wanting to get married to save hiring a man. They have to promise to support him before he will talk business." (Moore, 1981.)

Home life would improve. The typical pioneer went through at least three homes. The first drafty, dirt-floor log cabin yielded to a square-hewed log house, then finally to a bigger and more substantial home built of sawn lumber. Some who benefited from the smiles of financial fortune built castle-like houses on hillsides.

Life eventually eased for homemakers. "The way I got my washing machine was when I was carrying my second boy," recalled Betty Wilkinson in an interview about life in the 1930s. "He weighed twelve and a half

Lovely, sheltered valleys would not remain pristine forever, as early settlers carved homes and farms out of the wilderness. Here Albert Baker surveys his holdings on Winberry Creek, east of Lowell, about 1905. (Photo: Leppert.)

pounds. It took me two days and nights to deliver. Wayne [husband] did the washing twice, him and his mother. She made him wash on the board, and she'd throw 'em back if they weren't clean. The third washing, we got a washing machine." (Wilkinson.)

Lane County gained stature as a place to establish a farm and build a home. Poet Joaquin Miller spoke of his yearning for the green trees of home. In 1865 he revisited Eugene, his earlier hometown, and he spoke fondly of seeing "frisking lambs" and hearing "the myriad notes of the bullfrogs floating from afar. How I should like to live here and dream all the days of my life. Maybe I will sometime." ("Joaquin Miller.") He never did. But many others did, carving homes and ultimately communities out of the wilderness.

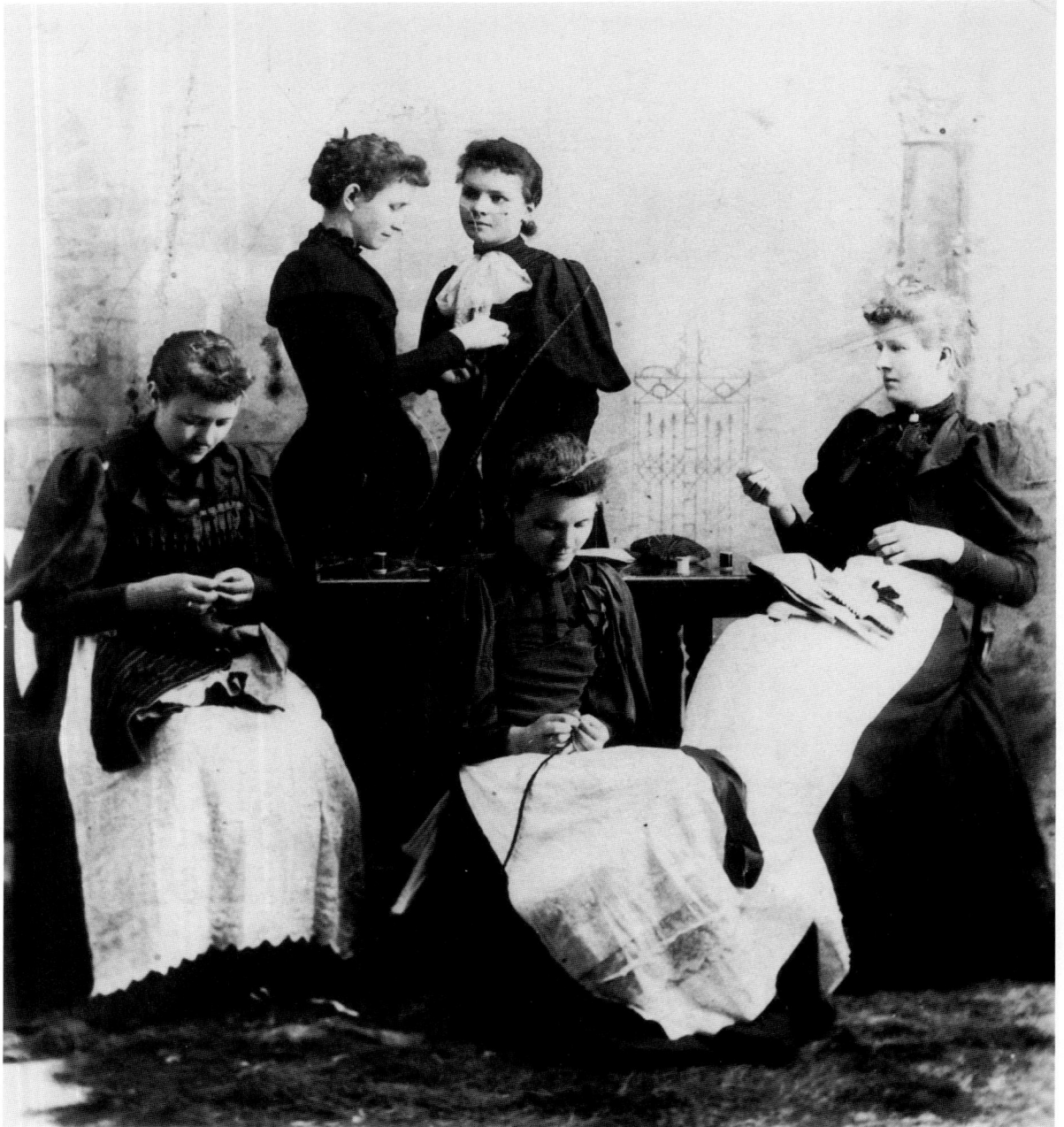

Ladies' sewing groups such as this one (about 1895) formed an important part of life. They met, worked on their mending, helped each other make dresses, and caught up on the neighborhood gossip.

Soap making, around 1915. The earliest home-made soap emerged from a simple if laborious process. First you filtered water through the ashes of several months of cooking stove fires. The process produced "lye water" which you poured into the iron kettle with animal fat rendered from cooking. If the fat was rancid and smelly, as it usually was without refrigeration, you added flower petals as perfume. Heat the kettle over a fire and stir with wooden paddle until the content attains the consistency of honey. Let dry and cure a couple of weeks before using.

Spinning wheel, 1908. The early day homemaker often made her own fabric, spinning wool into thread. Weaving thread into fabrics would eventually produce home-styled clothing. Spinning wheels came in various sizes from large standing wheels for wool yarns to smaller wheels for lighter threads.

Children at a logging camp school. Sometimes life was raw in the primitive schools situated deep in the woods. Clare Thurman recalled an experience in one such elementary school. One of her classmates hated school and wanted to be kicked out. "He'd eat garlic every day. It was awful. Then it came cold weather and he dropped some on the stove. I tell you we pretty near went crazy."

Protest at the "Wendling Stump," about 1900. The gentlemen pictured here moved to this new home after complaining about body lice infesting the bunkhouse at the Booth-Kelly mill at Wendling. (Photo: Henry R. Ross.)

Houses getting fancier: "Storybook castle" on the hill overlooking a snowy Eugene in 1910. In 1888, Dr. Thomas W. Shelton and his wife, Adah, built and moved into this house on the south slope of Skinner Butte in Eugene. Their daughter, Alberta, grew up here and the house served as the wedding site when she married Robert McMurphey, a businessman in 1893 (wedding shown at right; photo: Winter Photo Company). Drs. Eva and Curtis Johnson acquired the house in 1950 and deeded it to public domain in 1975. (Frankel.) The house remains a prominent historic landmark overlooking the railroad depot.

Eugene businessman C. S. Frank occupied this home by Eugene's Millrace, which gradually changed from an industrial to a recreational stream. The house, shown in 1900, survived until 1968.

No place like home for the holidays. Cozy home, tucked amid the tall trees of Eugene (East 11th and Hilyard), receives a visit from Fisher Laundry wagon in January 1909. (Photo: John Hartog.)

CHAPTER FOUR

Establishing a Community

IF IT WEREN'T FOR EMERGING pioneer communities, there would be no historical records. We would never have known the incorporation dates of Eugene (1862), Springfield (1885), Lowell (1954), or Westfir (1979). We would never have known countless landmark dates: arrival of electricity in Eugene (1887), telephones (1894 with 25 subscribers using hand-crank phones), and first automobile (1904). Nor would communities have developed public personas for intellectuals, writers, and critics to dwell on.

Eugene Skinner, of course, praised Oregon and the community he founded, the one that bears his first name.

"Could you but see our land of enchantment," he wrote to his sister in Canada in 1860. "The country is new, we have no aristocracy and no high style of living. Still we enjoy life as well as those who roll in luxuries*." (Lane County Historian*, Spring 1992.)

Poet Joaquin Miller, for all his talk about moving back to Eugene, expressed a less sanguine view to a national audience: "Eugene City, a dear, delightful town among the oaks, but slow and badly 'hide-bound.' Here are six great church buildings—never more than half-filled—and hardly two decent schoolhouses. Here is a great army of boys growing up, proficient chiefly in the mysteries of 'kissing-bees' and country dances. No trades, no professions, no education to speak of; nothing but helpless dependence on the 'old man.'" (Miller, 1872.)

Communities develop for the mutual benefit of the citizens. They start with a few farm houses, then acquire a trading post, a church, a blacksmith shop. Maybe a saloon. Then comes the need to educate children, and to raise funds to pay for a school and a teacher—and on it goes. Fire protection. Streets. Sidewalks, city hall, police, traffic enforcement, courthouse, sewers, jails, universities, hospitals, social services, and—taxes.

Civic matters were relatively simple at first. In 1876, when Eugene had about 1,100 population, records show that the city had spent $3,132.13 during the past fiscal year. The City Council discussed ways to "discover wherein expenses might be curtailed." But problems persisted. Hogs freely roamed the muddy streets, and the council had asked the town marshal to corral them. But the council hadn't discussed what to do with them once gathered. Members discussed building a "hog pound"—but could they afford the expense? (Walling, p. 407-8.)

Growing communities quickly acquire civic problems, all right. And the solution then as now is often more spending, higher taxes. Fortunately, in those days the populace had an excellent sense of humor. The standard joke of the era told of a group of hogs strolling down Willamette Street one day when one of them disappeared—down into the mud of the street, totally out of sight. Wasn't found until the following spring. Had a smile on his face when they dug him up.

FROM NORTH

Eventually isolated farm houses grew into rural communities. This is Lorane in 1910. Lorayne Kotrc and her brother, Rodney Dillon, recalled the thrill of venturing into the woods when they were kids. "I don't know why we kids didn't get lost," she said. "We always roamed these hills around here when they were all virgin timber. Folks never said anything just as long as we didn't get too close to where they were falling timber. We'd take a sandwich and take off to the brush. . . . It was pretty. We used to pick ladyslippers and take them to town and sell them for a nickel a bunch." (Edwards, p. 132.)

Scraped from the wilderness of the upper Willamette River: the beginnings of a town called Hazeldell, established in 1888. The name became Oakridge about six years before this 1916 photo was taken. The scene shows the essentials of a developing community (background, from left to right): school, hotel, residence, forestry office, and store-post office.

The early promise of a new community—will it grow and flourish into a major metropolis? Or will it languish in a backwater? This 1920 scene shows the community of Rainbow, on the McKenzie River between Blue River and McKenzie Bridge. Rainbow became a small, idyllic retreat along the river. (Photo: E. F. Martin.)

Early Lane County schools occupied log cabins, box cars, and homes. Few matched this Junction City School for architectural elegance, shown about 1914. Here the Barker family takes an excursion. Chris Wilde recalled an experience at this school in 1915. Elizabeth McKnight, the school superintendent's freckle-faced, long-haired daughter, occupied the desk in front of him. "One day her long, prolific red curls got into my ink bottle. I will never forget the hand spanking Mr. McKnight administered to my rear end while draped over a school desk in the east upstairs cloakroom." (Wilde, p. 99-100.)

On the Boardwalk at Glenada. Bustling waterfront town flourishes across the Siuslaw River from Florence on the Oregon coast in this 1914 photo. Over subsequent years, though, growth tended to favor Florence.

A case history on how Lane County's communities developed. Mapleton, originally called Seaton, flourished because it was the farthest inland large vessels could navigate upstream on the Siuslaw River. A brisk ferry business developed. People traveled by stagecoach from Eugene to Mapleton (perhaps overnight at the hotel), then down the river by boat to Florence and the Oregon coast. Photo taken about 1910.

A 1914 view of Eugene from Skinner Butte looking south along Willamette Street. Several of those buildings have survived—notably the Lane Hotel (foreground, right of Willamette) and the Eugene Electric Station (across Willamette from hotel). The U. S. Post Office replaced the livery stable behind the hotel.

View looking west from Judkins Point toward Eugene. University of Oregon campus on left, Willamette River and Skinner Butte on right.

About 1851 business leader
Hilyard Shaw cut and
shaped this Millrace in
Eugene from a flood
channel of the nearby
Willamette River. It powered
the industry of a city for
more than half a century
before this 1908 scene,
including the excelsior mill,
flour mill, woolen mill, and
cider mill shown here. When
no longer needed for power,
it became a recreational
stream, fabled in story and
song by generations of
students from the nearby
University of Oregon. A
college man with a canoe
enjoyed great popularity
with the ladies, said one
observer. (Tweedell. Photo:
John Hartog.)

Flood of Feb. 4th 1890

Water everywhere. Before dams controlled the Willamette, McKenzie, and other upstream tributaries, you could expect frequent floods in the Willamette Valley. These scenes are typical. (Above) Willamette River of February, 1890. Except for the north section, this bridge, the first Ferry Street Bridge in Eugene, withstood the flood while most of the covered bridges across the Willamette succumbed to the roiling waters. (Photo: Winter Photo Company.) (Opposite) Scene of a 1925 flood, location unknown.

Fire, deadly and often uncontrollable, became the scourge of early communities. Here in this August 1934 photo, roaring flames engulf a sawmill in Oakridge. (Photo: Willamette National Forest.)

AN OREGON SAPLIN

CHAPTER **FIVE**

Working

GIVEN THE EXTREME GEOGRAPHIC DIVERSITY of Lane County, it should come as no surprise that working was dominated by occupations close to the land. Forget the new trends toward high technology. Few, if any, photos have yet worked their way into the county's historical museums to show the manufacture of compact disks or computer chips. Wood chips, yes.

So archival photos of working people are mostly of men, especially men in dramatic outdoor occupations such as logging or releasing a carrier pigeon from a 10,000-foot mountain. Women appear occasionally in the farm fields, particularly harvesting hops, and in service occupations such as nursing, teaching, and telephone communications. Even those are rare, as early photos donated to museum archives tended to represent high drama against spectacular scenery.

Whatever those considerations, the history of work in this region is fairly simple, and it follows the lay of the land. Forests cover fully 88 percent of Lane County, according to the *Atlas of Lane County, Oregon*, so it is natural that work related to the woods has dominated the photo archives: logging, sawmilling, forest maintenance. Of the remaining 12 percent, three-fourths is agricultural (crops and rangeland). So agriculture ranked second both in the

economy and in the photo collections. What remains of the land is mostly barren (sand dunes, rocks, glacial ice, lava fields: 2% of the total). Urbanized land represents a mere one percent.

As for work, some conditions clearly are changing in Lane County, a point worthy of mention to sort matters into proper historical context.

One of the county's first female log truck drivers, Karen Inman, said in an interview taped by a university graduate student in 1989: "At the beginning, the men thought I was out there trying to take a man's job. When they found out that I was supporting myself and my family, then they respected me for it because I wasn't on welfare as I could have been." With no background in driving, she had a lot to learn. "You have to learn about engines. . . about tires. And your trailer, how to take it off and hook it up."

In another excerpt, Robert Crump described himself as one of the last of the old-growth timber fallers. "When I was cutting old-growth fir I'd go home at night if I had something that was really challenging me mentally—a big tree in a bad area and trying to decide where to put that tree as far as what lay to fall it into and save the tree. . . . It's like a jigsaw puzzle, being able to cross your timber and pick your ground. Now there's no mental work involved. You go out and fall a tree and you go on to the next one. It's all mechanized logging now." (Weiss.)

These photos, then, show how it was in past years.

No doubt about it—work in the historical context meant logging and lumbering in Lane County. The industry also attracted photographers, drawn by its outdoor flavor, scenic grandeur, economic importance, and high drama. Here is a 1910 woods scene in Lane County, precise location unknown. You won't see many Douglas fir trees this size anymore: eight to ten feet in diameter. Hard hats were unknown then. Dangers abounded in the big woods, but men drew pride in felling a tree this big. Many preferred logging to the common alternative, sawmill work, perceiving the outdoor work healthier, less routine, more exciting.

Roy Hills rides a log through the rapids at Black Canyon on the Willamette River downstream from Oakridge, about 1905. On river drives to the mills, logs often stuck on rocks and river bends, producing huge jams. Historian Hallie Huntington wrote: "Jam breakers had the delicate footwork of a ballerina. They skipped lightly from log to log, where a miscalculation or a slip of the carefully caulked boots would have plunged them into the log jam and almost certain death." (Huntington, 1984, p. 71.)

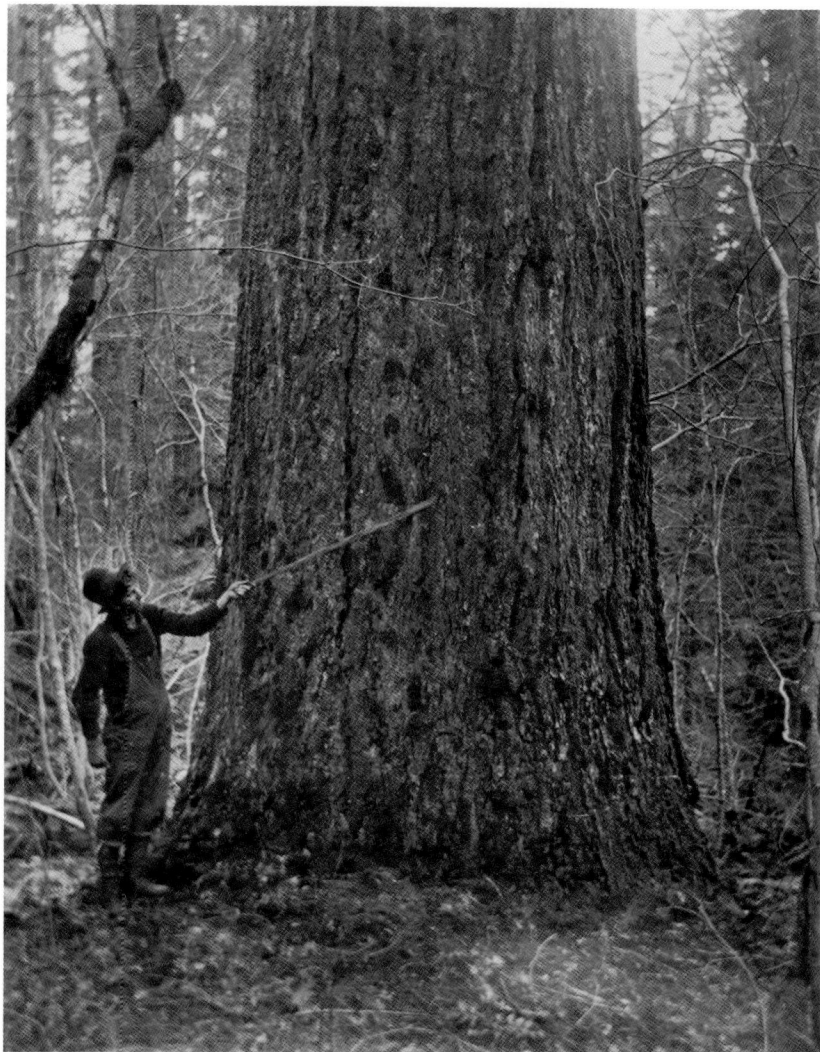

Giant old growth Douglas fir, the best of timber and a
challenge to the loggers, date unknown. A depression-era
logger, Guy Virgin, explained the preference for big trees:
"In the woods they only took the choicest logs. . . . If the tree
had a little speck of rot on it, they would leave it."
(Photo: Henry R. Ross.)

Hauling heavy logs out of the woods to a place where they could be dispatched to the sawmill was a problem for early lumbermen. One solution, shown in this circa 1900 photo, was the high wheel to which the logs were lashed. This eventually gave way to more advanced technology.

The pole road served to transport logs down steep inclines to the mills, as shown in this Booth-Kelly logging operation about 1901. (Photo: Henry R. Ross.)

Horses on the job pulling logs,
Jones Lumber Company near
Saginaw, about 1895.

Steam donkeys became an essential part of the logging process, used to pull logs from the falling areas to the waiting rail cars (later trucks) destined for the mill. This donkey, near Cottage Grove, is literally pulling itself uphill to a new location, date unknown.

Giant logs are loaded onto a rail car
at the Booth-Kelly logging operation
near Wendling, about 1908.

Ingenious devices often served to haul logs out of the woods. Forests above Oakridge stood on rugged terrain. This steep railroad "incline," as it was called, served to move logs to the Westfir Lumber Company. A log truck driver, Wesley "Red" Clark, working there about 1938, recalled: "The incline was a railroad track built right up the side of a mountain, up onto what they call High Prairie. And it was 77 percent, straight up the side of the canyon. And they had a huge donkey at the top. . . with about a two-and-a-half-inch cable that they would hook onto those loads of logs and let them down the incline with this big machine, down to meet this other railroad that ran up the North Fork. And then they'd pull the empties back up. . . . They had lots of trouble with that incline. I've heard stories that when one of those'd get away, those 88-foot logs would go end over end down that slope." (Metzler. Photo: Oakridge Pioneer Museum collection.)

A locomotive pulls logs through the snow out of the woods
to the mill, about 1900; location unknown.

Lumber for farmers. Here's the Mohawk Lumber Company, northeast of Springfield, with masses of sawn lumber awaiting shipment, about 1913. Much of this lumber went into houses and farm buildings around Harrisburg where the company maintained a retail outlet.

Early Lane County sawmills such as this one (about 1910, location unknown) sold much of their lumber to local markets, hauling by wagon to retail lumber yards in the nearby communities. Railroads also carried lumber shipments, particularly to locations farther afield, such as California markets.

By 1940, plywood—sheets of peeled veneer glued together at various thicknesses—was becoming a burgeoning industry that would serve during the forthcoming World War II and long after. This is the Springfield Plywood Corporation, July 27, 1940. (Photo: Kennell-Ellis.)

1888

SHIPPING SCENE ON SIUSLAW.

Lane County products also went by sea from the Florence area. Lumber schooners are being towed to sea across the Siuslaw River bar (above)—or, in the photo at the top, under full sail. Steam and gas vessels gradually replaced the sailer. From 1900 through 1903, 169 sailers and 129 steamers called at Siuslaw docks, leaving with 31 million feet of lumber, enough to build 2,000 homes. Most of the lumber went to the San Francisco area. (Lomax, 1971. Photos: Siuslaw Pioneer Museum collection.)

Windjammer at dockside. A schooner loads lumber at dock on the Siuslaw River at Florence in this 1910 scene. Canned salmon was also loaded on these ships, which plied the coastal route between Oregon ports and San Francisco.

Milk deliveries in 1910. The men were employed by the
Tom Walker cheese factory, Pleasant Hill.

Threshing wheat on the Fred and Annie Wright ranch at Walker, between Cottage
Grove and Creswell, about 1909. Coming at the end of summer, threshing was hot,
tedious work often dawn to dusk. A steam-powered tractor ran threshing machine
which separated straw from grain, the latter to be hauled to storage and eventual
sale. Anne Thomas wrote: "The neighborhood farmers would work together,
threshing all the grain on one farm, then moving to the next farm. . . . When the
threshing crew was working on a farm, the housewife was expected to feed the
whole crew of approximately 15 men." (Thomas.)

Picking Hops at the Barbre Hop Yard, Fall Creek, about 1905. Working in the hop yards, recalled Chris Wilde of Junction City, "was a vacation for most people: romance as well as sweat and toil. The teenagers looked forward to the night time, when around the campfire they would sing songs. . . . One full moonlit night a hop flatbed wagon, loaded with youth, was driving back from the campfire when they saw a tightly clasped standing couple in grain stubble a hundred feet west of the gravel road. . . . How they hollered! I should know; I was the Romeo at age 16." (Wilde, p. 288.)

Peaches were prominent among the agricultural crops produced in Lane County. This 1913 scene shows the peach harvest on the John Thramer farm on the Willamette River, a site whose soil was often enriched by loam deposited by the flooding river. Upstream dams constructed in the 1950s controlled the frequent floods, and the site eventually became a Eugene city park—Alton Baker Park, named for the longtime publisher of Eugene's daily newspaper, *The Register-Guard.*

A mountain of flax emerges from harvest activities on this unidentified Lane County farm, about 1940. Flax production flourished briefly when unsettled conditions before and during World War II interrupted the export of European flax. Willamette Valley growing conditions were perfect for flax, and 14 processing plants quickly emerged, three of them in Lane County. Flax served wartime military needs such as parachute harnesses, fire hoses, bomb slings, signal halyards, and many others. (Wyatt.)

Cutting a railroad tunnel—the hard way. Pick and
sledgehammer, and a fair amount of brawn, served to cut a
tunnel through solid rock, about 1912.

Wagons loading gravel at the Eugene Sand and Gravel
Company, about 1904. This site was at the north end of High
Street in Eugene by the Willamette River.

Need for new roads in Lane County put men and animals on the job, which was labor intensive in early days. This construction crew is working on the Crow Road, a mile east of Territorial Highway, about 1921.

Daring high-beam act. Workmen on the scaffolding as they near completion of the steel bridge over the Willamette River between Eugene and Springfield in 1890. (Photo: Winter Photo Company.)

Before the days of the supermarket, grocery stores like this served Lane County shoppers. Grocery clerks are ready to help shoppers find what they want. This is the Kearny Groceteria on West Broadway, Eugene, about 1929.

In contrast to the hearty workers in the woods, the mills, the farms, and the commercial fishing vessels, bankers had a relatively comfortable work environment, only occasionally enlivened by armed robbers. This is the Lane County Bank on the corner of Eighth Avenue and Willamette Street in Eugene, 1903. Banking got off to an uneven start at first, as most settlers, not especially trusting, preferred to stash their money in old cans or out in the wood pile. But by 1903 banking was well established in Lane County.

A high-level position. In the 1920s the Forest Service experimented with carrier pigeons to carry messages, particularly those related to fire lookout activity. Here a forester releases a pigeon from Oregon's third highest peak, the South Sister. Lookouts came to use more dependable two-way telephone communications and eventually radio. (Photo: Willamette National Forest.)

CHAPTER SIX

Getting Around

OF ALL THE CONVEYANCES for getting around, none is more bizarre than riding a flume out of the woods. This is not a gag shot. Woods and mill workers actually did ride flumes—given the need for a quick departure, it was often either that or walk. Perhaps you can see why logging became one of the most dangerous occupations on record.

In today's era when residents of the southern Willamette Valley can reach either the Pacific Ocean or the Cascade Mountains in an hour, the earlier problems of getting around in Lane County may seem astonishing.

When the T. G. Hendricks and F. M. Wilkins families—prominent early names in Eugene—decided to travel to the coast in 1892 for two or three weeks, getting there meant four or five days of travel by horse-drawn vehicles. They moved tediously by trail to Mapleton, the head of tidewater on the Siuslaw River. They then sailed by ferry to Florence. They traveled north about ten miles to a campsite by Lily Lake. From there they continued four miles to the beach below Heceta Head where the famous lighthouse was then under construction. Getting there definitely was *not* half the fun.

Yet, as the photos on these pages suggest, matters did improve. Railroads came, streetcars came, and eventually the automobile came. "The car was a big threat when it came," recalled Clarence Pitney of Junction City who gave a taped interview in 1975. "But it was a big advantage, too. I remember my brother was raking hay with a little dump rig when one of those contraptions came down the road and scared the horse. He ran off and kicked my brother's shin and laid several inches wide open. The doctor came out from Junction City in a runabout which cranked from the side. I asked him how fast he came, and he said, 'Oh, about 15 miles an hour.' Well, we didn't laugh at that. We thought that was doing pretty good!" (*Season of Harvest*, p. 103.)

The auto was no panacea. If Lane County ranks high for rainfall, it ranks equally high for mud. Museum photos of cars traversing axle-deep mud (and often getting stuck) are common. Roads were largely wagon trails: rutted, muddy, and often blocked by downed trees and slides. And dusty in summer. You also could plan on three or four flat tires in a 40-mile adventure. Yet the old Ford Model-T, standing high off the ground compared to current vehicles, was surprisingly dependable for getting out of tight spots. Even so, many residents remained reluctant to give up what they considered the best transportation of early times—a single horse and rider. The second best probably was the bicycle.

The logging flume was hardly designed for passenger comfort but rather for freight. This scene shows a Booth-Kelly operation at Saginaw about 1901. The B-K flume served to ship rough-cut "cants" to a second mill for resawing and planing. (Photo: Henry R. Ross.)

Eugene's first streetcar, about 1893, mule-powered, run by a conductor known as "Old Wiley." Top speed six miles per hour. "Old Wiley hitched his mule to the end of the streetcar according to which way it was headed. . . . . He carried candy for children who saved their pennies until they had five cents, then they rode the streetcar all the way to the university and walked home." (Huntington, 1994.)

Bicycling began in Eugene at an early year, and the community became a national leader in development of bicycle pathways, especially those along the Willamette River through town. This photo shows Frank L. Chambers and Ida Chambers, with their daughter, Mary, on a bicycle in front of their home about 1897. Ida died a few years after this photo was made. Frank became a prominent businessman. Mary lived to the age of 102 (died 1996).

Among the transportation alternatives was the ferry. The *Hazel* with passenger-laden barge alongside, crosses the Siuslaw Bay by Florence. (Photo: Siuslaw Pioneer Museum collection.)

With bicycles aboard for exploration and perhaps for the return trip back upstream, a party launches this rowboat in the Willamette River upstream from the Ferry Street Bridge in Eugene around 1905.

Various means of early transportation at Fifth and Willamette in Eugene. This scene, about 1913, features horse-drawn buggy, automobile, pedestrians, and—most particularly—the new, modern electric train running regular schedules north to Portland. The landmark Oregon Electric Depot remains to this day, as a restaurant with dining in antique rail cars.

The Cottage Grove Southern Pacific station (opposite) about 1910. In 1960, Herbert Thompson recalled several early train rides to Portland with his family, starting in 1880 when he was five. "We boys were too busy looking out the window to talk. There was nothing ugly or dull on that ride—no dismal factory towns and nothing commonplace. It was all clear, clean countryside with grain farms, views of hills, stands of virgin timber, some views of the river, a fine one of Oregon City Falls." (Thompson.)

The train opened new horizons. At Irving, north of Eugene, a passenger awaits the train to Portland, about 1905. Station manager awaits train's arrival with mail sack and lady's valise in hand.

By 1910, Eugene had emerged as a cosmopolitan city, complete with streetcar lines running all the way to Springfield. Electric-powered trolleys arrived in Eugene in 1907 and expanded to Springfield in 1910. Proclaimed the *Eugene Guard*: "Amid the shrieking of mill whistles, the enthusiastic and tremendous cheering of the crowd assembled in Springfield, the first streetcar bearing 125 Eugene boosters rolled across the new bridge this morning, marking a new epoch in the growth of this country." By 1927, the streetcar era was over, replaced by buses and private autos. (Hulin.)

McKenzie River and Highway

Cruising the Oregon byways around Oakridge in 1921. Lawrence Hills, grandson of Oregon Trail pioneer Cornelius Hills, and wife Vera happily explore the countryside.

The Cadillac of early day autos—quite a spectacle at the time of this photo in Springfield, about 1908. Autos would proliferate, and within ten years Lane County Sheriff Dillard A. Elkins would complain about cars exceeding the speed limits, 25 mph on highways and 16 mph in the city: "This speeding has got to be stopped. The team or pedestrian has rights on the roads just the same as the motorist, and these rights must be respected." (*Eugene Guard*, June 13, 1918. Photo: Smith Mountjoy.)

The auto encouraged exploration, but it wasn't easy negotiating the precarious "highway" along the McKenzie River around 1925. Finn Rock, the monolith in the center, bears the name of Benjamin Franklin "Huckleberry" Finn, pioneer settler who called himself the "Biggest damned liar on the McKenzie River." He claimed to be the inspiration for Mark Twain's *Huckleberry Finn*. Some folks dispute his claim that this big rock originally stood on the other side of the river. He said he had secured wet rawhide around it and tied the other end to a tree on shore. When the sun came out it dried and tightened the rawhide—and soon, "over come the rock." (Photo: Smith Mountjoy.)

Mahlon Sweet, Eugene auto dealer, civic leader, and aviation pioneer, cruises across the Pass Creek Canyon Road between Eugene and Roseburg. The year is 1911. Sweet was one of the county's foremost transportation pioneers. He opened a car dealership in Eugene and served on a committee to develop better roads in Oregon. In 1919 the Legislature established a tax on gas to pay for roads. "Get Oregon out of the mud" became the motto. It was the first such tax in the nation. Long interested in air travel, Sweet worked to develop a "super airport" for Eugene, which opened in 1943 as Mahlon Sweet Field.

Mountain adventures. On the Oregon Stage bus, McKenzie Pass, eastern Lane County. A delightful prospect in summer (right, about 1930; North and Middle Sister in the background), but perhaps a trifle bleak in winter (above, about 1927). Highway crews no longer maintain the McKenzie Pass in winter. (Photos: Chester Stevenson.)

Carving pathways and bridges out of the Oregon wilderness (opposite) left driving a little precarious. Bridges without railings required caution and steady nerves. But the woodsy scenery was magnificent and traffic not unbearably heavy. This 1920 scene shows a wooden bridge near McCredie Springs on the Willamette Pass.

Game Creek
McCready Springs

Nels Roney, a contractor famed for his bridge building in Lane County, erected this 215-foot span in 1874 and painted it red, his color of choice for bridges. It was the second major bridge built in Lane County. For 53 years it served at the Hayden Bridge crossing of the McKenzie River north of Springfield. The railroad bridge appears in the background of this scene, photographed about 1921. Covered spans like this gained the informal name "kissing bridges" in recognition of activities alleged to have occurred there at night with a romantic patter of rain on the roof. (Photo: Smith Mountjoy.)

City driving was often precarious when drenching rains descended. Even as late as 1916, date of this view on East 12th Avenue, "Skinner's Mudhole" remained an appropriate if derisive nickname for the community Eugene Skinner had founded.

An historic occasion at the Eugene Air Park September 27, 1924. The Air Park on 19th and Chambers was Oregon's only municipally owned field then, and these Army Air Corps aviators chose it as their last overnight stop before completing a dramatic round-the-world flight at Seattle the following day. At the end, they had traveled 27,524 miles through 29 countries in 176 days. Of the four planes departing Seattle the previous April, one crashed in Alaska and another ditched in the Atlantic Ocean. The crews survived. Lieutenant Lowell H. Smith (standing third from right) considered himself a Lane County man, having spent three previous summers in Eugene as commander of the forest fire patrols over Oregon, whose pilots were provided by the Air Corps. He told an evening banquet audience that he was "anxious to get back to Lane County for a deer hunt."

Aircraft era begins: "Eugene No. 1," about 1920. Was this Eugene's first airplane? The record is unclear, but R. A. McCully and R. H. Pierce purchased the first airplane and used it commercially for two years, charging $15 for a 15-minute ride.

Around 1918, the penalties for careless driving were swift and troublesome. The lucky drivers needed only to change tires. In an interview Dave Walp said: "I can remember that the first trip I ever made up the river was in 1917 in an old Studebaker automobile. It was an all-day trip .... You'd probably have three or four flat tires between Eugene and Belknap Springs." (*Season of Harvest,* p. 19.)

The new railroad technology did not, of course, always work smoothly. This engine went off the track at Walker Siding between Cottage Grove and Creswell about 1905. The train was enroute to Portland.

At least dad salvaged a lantern after this 1915 mishap.

Sometimes the new horseless carriage was known to venture out of its element, with predictable results. (Photo: Siuslaw Pioneer Museum collection.)

CHAPTER SEVEN

Entertainment

Home entertainment, pioneer style. The Neely family, living near Florence, makes its own entertainment around 1910 with organ-violin duet by a cozy fireplace.

WHAT, NO TELEVISION? How grim. Yet, from published diaries and taped accounts, bygone eras seemed more sociable, more *civilized* than today. "I think our lives—other than being without electricity and things—were wonderful," declared Melvina Neet. "We were close together. We didn't have anything to do in the evenings, you know—no radio, no television, no nothing. So we'd light our old coal oil lantern and go to the neighbors and spend the evening. Then they'd light up their old lantern and come and return the visit."

People often made their own entertainment during winter evenings around a fireplace. Travel, though often difficult, led to scenic wonders—river banks, swimming holes, hot springs, fishing sites. Residents flocked to civic celebrations, especially on the Fourth of July. Bands played, troops marched, orators harangued. Folks picnicked and entered contests: foot races, sack races, even ladies' nail driving contests.

"We had dances where everybody in the neighborhood went," recalled Bessie Raymond. "We would get in the wagon or bobsled and go down, spend the whole night dancing."

Bill Bartels recalled: "The movies in those days would show train robberies. . . . I'd go

see it over and over. Quite a thrill! . . . . Old Man Goodrich had a rattle box [radio]. We listened to the Hoot Owls. Every once in awhile we'd listen, about one or two o'clock in the morning, to Chicago. We could hear just a little bit, you know, and, oh, boy. That was quite a thing!" (*Season of Harvest*, 1975.)

Kids of yesteryear fashioned their own entertainment. Bud Hall, who grew up in the remote lumber town of Wendling, prepared a list of "58 fun things to do"—from "kick the can" with an empty Pet milk container to passing Curly Bailey's picket fence on your bike and rattling the pickets with a stick. "Be out of sight before Curly came racing out the door." (Byers.)

When kids grew to adulthood, entertainment assumed a new meaning. The 1875 diary of a 19-year-old belle reflected on an incident at a dance with a young man referred to as "C." He'd given her a piece of candy bearing five inscribed words.

"I am afraid I'm not treating him right," wrote Jessie Hills. "A while back I fear I was not treating him well enough, now I'm afraid I'm treating him too well. I look at him too often, always meet his glance with a smile. . . . The words were *'tis you alone I love*. 'Can you read it?' he asked. 'Yes, but I don't believe it,' said I. 'You don't believe it?' he repeated, looking into my eyes with a glance that made my heart beat. 'No,' with a saucy laugh. A little later his nose began to bleed." ("Cornelius Hills Family," p. 54.)

Note: Jessie Hills, who, as her diary makes clear, had lots of beaus, eventually married Charlie Humphreys, probably the "C" mentioned in the diary. Jessie was the daughter of pioneer immigrant Cornelius Hills, patriarch of a Lane County family dynasty.

Fourth of July festivities at the lumber community of Marcola in 1904. Foot races were a common spectacle at celebrations like this, including kids' races and three-legged races. Even the women raced in their long dresses. (Photo: Henry R. Ross.)

Having fun is easy when you're young: (above) Getting ready for the Bicycle Days festivities in Coburg in 1902 (photo: J. Merle Nighswander); (left) frolicking on the swings while getting ready for a picture in Oakridge about 1916; (opposite, top) Indian children amusing themselves at Seavey Hop Yards while parents work, about 1910; and (opposite, bottom) "smoking" cottonwood sticks ("balm") about 1911.

The bands played on: (above) The Junction City Band about 1890; (opposite, bottom) the brass band from the community of Crow playing at nearby Lorane about 1901; and (opposite, top) a band at the Lane County Fairgrounds about 1925. (Photo: E. F. Martin.)

Adventuring in river country. The railroad view (above) is dated about 1885 at Coryell Pass, located on the Willamette River near its junction with the coast fork. (Photo: Rhinehart.) In the 1910 view below, autos assume more importance in the lives of residents eager to explore primitive roads to discover enchanting Willamette River scenes.

An outing by car and ferry, about 1911. This was the Harrisburg Ferry on the Willamette River, crossing between Linn and Lane Counties. It had its share of dramatic events through the years. One time a team of horses carrying a heavy wagon panicked on the steep ferry approach at Harrisburg and ran across the vessel, plunging over the end into 16 feet of water. Quick thinking by handlers released them from the wagon and averted a drowning. Years later a carload of Portlanders drove down the ramp to the ferry landing one dark night—but the ferry was across the river at the time. Later the skeletal remains of the victims were among rocks scooped up by a downstream gravel plant. (Wilde, p. 271. Photo: Smith Mountjoy).

Heceta Head on the coast about 1912. The new lighthouse
in the background was destined to be one of the Oregon
coast's most-photographed scenes. No record exists to tell
what the bathing beauties are up to, precisely—perhaps
pretending to be stranded on a desert islet awash in the
incoming surf.

Hunting-fishing party at woods camp, date and location unknown. For some, hunting was more than entertainment. "I've hunted since I was knee-high to a grasshopper." said Frank Baker of Oakridge. "Used to hunt because that's all we had to eat. . . . There wasn't no work, just didn't have anything. Trouble was in them days we couldn't get ammunition. Didn't have the money to buy it." (*Season of Harvest*. Photo: Charles Weaver.)

For many men, having a good time meant getting away from it all, away from civilization and into the wilderness. This 1922 hunting party is departing McKenzie Bridge for an extended hunting trip to Indian Ridge, a long ride up the McKenzie River's south fork.

Relaxing on the summit of one of the Three Sisters, previously named Faith, Hope, and Charity. About 1892. Pioneer climber Thomas Judkins recalled the feeling of the last few steps: "Step after step, 10, 20, 100 feet then look up. Another 100 feet and another look. Now we sniff breezes from the summit. Our steps are longer. The burdens seem to fall from our shoulders. We shout, we halt. Our feet are planted on the highest rock of Hope, over 10,000 feet above the level of the sea." (Photo: Winter Photo Company.)

McAllister Rapids, McKenzie River, 1939. A boat trip on the McKenzie meant whitewater thrills and fishing. "A trip of four or five miles was enough to fairly load the boat with fish," recalled early river guide Prince Helfrich. "When Martin Rapids was reached, the boat was lined around. It was not until about 1924 that daring guides started running the rapids, and then without passengers. In those days it was necessary to carry a big water bucket for bailing after running the rapids. . . in such places as Clover Point, Martin, McAllister, and Gate Creek. And if a guide came in at the end of the day not soaking wet to the waist, he had not put in much of a day." (Helfrich, p. 17. Photo: Howard.)

Climbers ascending one of the Three Sisters, about 1898. From the earliest years, the high country proved attractive to adventurous residents. Thomas Judkins had made such a climb years earlier and described the ordeal: "Over ice and snow and streamlets. On, over fastnesses to which we are strangers. On, over the backbone of a forbidding ridge. Just here we must move very slowly for a mis-step might hurl us headlong downward."

Hangin' out by the drug store, South
River Road, Cottage Grove, about 1900.

Formal night out in Eugene about
1890: a touch of elegance indoors,
and a refuge from the outdoor scene
where the streets were often muddy
and the rivers sometimes overflowed.
This dance took place in Rhinehart's
Hall, corner of East Ninth Avenue and
Oak Street. (Photo: Winter Photo
Company.)

Sometimes entertainment in 1900 was little more than meeting someone on the street on a sunny day and having a chat—perhaps about old times, perhaps about politics. On the right stands Oregon's first governor, John Whiteaker, of Eugene. Elected in 1858, he served until 1862.

Entertainment was where you found it. Outside the Bohemia Saloon in Cottage Grove about 1915, gentlemen line the wooden sidewalk to inspect this animal, said to be the first Hereford bull in the community.

CHAPTER EIGHT

The Last Settler

Three Sisters
Wilderness Area,
eastern Lane
County, 1962.
(Photo: Willamette
National Forest.)

WHAT OF THE FUTURE OF LANE COUNTY? Asked that question in the 1930s, Sam Boardman might have suggested it for a state park. Boardman, as Oregon's first state parks superintendent, acquired park properties at a rate unparalleled in any other state. Lane County's coastal Honeyman Park was a Boardman acquisition. Soon after his appointment, he announced that he'd staked out his first park. It extended from the Cascade Mountains to the sea and from the Columbia River to the California border. Tongue in cheek, of course—this Massachusetts immigrant wanted merely to call attention to the scenic grandeur of the western third of Oregon.

This was nothing new. Testimonials have long extolled the beauty of Oregon and Lane County.

"Look at the Cascades with its dark brow of evergreen and beautiful hills," Joaquin Miller wrote in the *Eugene City Review* in 1862. "Look at the little knolls and buttes that lay stretched up and down the valley, covered with white flocks and fat herds, and listen to the foaming sea afar off that beats with eternal roar over rockbound shores. And tell me if this, our sunset home, is not a land of song and beauty."

The sunset photo on the opposite page seems equally lyrical, perhaps a metaphor for the region. Trees in the foreground imply an unseen forest beyond, with a dark cloud fringed by a silver lining and a ray of hope projecting outward.

"The first settlers believed Oregon to be a kind of Eden," declared historian Terrence O'Donnell writing in the *Oregon Blue Book*. "Now, a century and a half later, their descendants appear determined that it remain so."

In that context we complain about growth, too many immigrants on the latter-day Oregon Trails—I-84 and I-5. Nothing new here. Through the past 150 years the last settler to arrive in Eden has wanted to close the gates and not let anyone else in. Historians call it the "Last Settler Syndrome."

Failing to lock the gates, this strictly Oregon attitude prevails nonetheless. It leads to laws such as the state's stringent land-use regulations which encourage growth within urban boundaries but protect the land beyond from wanton development. One study by a national agency proclaimed the program a great success, but added that it could succeed in no other state but Oregon.

Latter-day scene shows Waldo Lake still a monument to pristine beauty, though in recent years more accessible (but guarded by mosquitoes in early summer). (Photo: Tonya Houg, Willamette National Forest, 1979.)

It is heartening, in any event, to know that not everyone loves Lane County. In the remote mountain community of Deadwood, Miss Green arrived in the early 1900s to teach at the elementary school. A petite young woman less than five feet tall, she found the strapping young schoolboys intimidating, especially when they put snakes in her lunchbox. She promptly retreated to her home in eastern Oregon. ("Elnans of Deadwood.") ◆

General Joseph Lane, about 1875.

CHAPTER NINE

A Compact History of Lane County

E ONS PASSED before the land was ready for people. Not until the sea receded, land masses shifted, and mountain ranges thrust upward did it take shape. Volcanoes erupted, lava flows and glaciation molded lakes, rivers carved pathways to the sea. Time passed and conifers grew near the streams. Forests and flower-strewn mountain meadows appeared, and grass carpeted the valley floor. Only then did the people come.

Indians, or Native Americans as we now call them, arrived first. Several different bands lived under the broad umbrella of two dominant tribes. The Calapooyas stayed mainly in the valley, living on berries, camasroots, and game. The Siuslaws lived on the coast, harvesting fish and shellfish from the sea. Other tribes, Molalla, Umpqua, Klamath, and Rogue, made frequent forays into the area.

Fire served as the tribes' most important possession. The Calapooyas—the region's first field burners—charred the fields in late summer to cluster the game animals, roast insects and small rodents, and prevent the prairies from reverting to forest.

Sadly, the number of Native Americans rapidly declined due to the onset of diseases such as smallpox, measles, and influenza introduced by the arrival of the white man after the beginning of the 19th Century. The first white men to explore what eventually became Lane County belonged to the Hudson's Bay Company, and they were searching for beaver. They took so many pelts that by the time they left the beaver was nearly extinct. Two trapper-explorers

are especially noteworthy. In 1812 Donald McKenzie, from John Jacob Astor's Pacific Fur Company, explored and hunted beaver through a river drainage that eventually acquired his name, the McKenzie River. Scotland-born David Douglas, a professional botanist, explored the region in 1826. The most important tree in Lane County bears his name: the Douglas fir. As the Hudson's Bay era waned, migration to the west steadily increased, reaching its peak in the 1850s.

In 1846 the first four white settlers arrived in Lane County: Eugene Skinner, Elijah Bristow, William Dodson, and Felix Scott. Bristow, Dodson, and Scott settled in the Pleasant Hill area. In 1850 a church and school, built on land donated by Bristow, formed the beginning of a community. Pleasant Hill remains as School District #1. Skinner settled by the butte that bears his name and soon planned a townsite.

Meanwhile, in 1848, the U. S. Congress passed a bill creating the Oregon Territory. General Joseph Lane served as Oregon's first territorial governor, a job turned down by Abraham Lincoln. Contemporaries described Lane as "not a large man, but well-knit, tough and wiry, with a lively and ambitious disposition." Known for his even-handed treatment of the Indians, he became a popular governor for the year he served. However, he was removed from office with the election of Whig President Zachary Taylor.

Lane remained active. During the Civil War he vigorously supported the south. This won him many enemies, including the press who called him "The old traitor, Jo Lane." He tried his hand at mining and other activities, then retired to his farm at Roseburg until his death in 1881 at 80.

In 1851 the Territorial Legislature passed an act to create and organize a county named after Joseph Lane, an appropriate action, as it turned out. The county, like its namesake, has often been at odds politically with other parts of the country. Eugene was chosen as the county seat.

The early boundaries of the new county were unclear—simply defined as "all that portion of Oregon lying south of Linn County and south of so much of Benton County as is east of the Umpqua." The definition failed to mention an eastern boundary; presumably it extended to the Rocky Mountains.

In 1853 the Territorial Legislature defined the southern boundary and clarified the eastern boundary: "Southerly to the summit of the Calapooya Mountains, thence eastward along the summit of said mountains to the summit of the Cascade Range."

Thus was created Lane County, a scenic splendor and unique among Oregon's 36 counties for its wide west-east stretch from sea level to mountains ranging beyond 10,000 feet. The country between offers gently rolling hills, prime agricultural land, and numerous lakes and streams.

The three dominant rivers are the Siuslaw, meandering through lush farm lands and thick forests to the ocean; the Willamette, winding northward through the valley that bears its name; and the McKenzie, noted for its icy, clear blue-green waters, swirling rapids, and breathtaking waterfalls.

Settlers had been making the overland journey westward in increasing numbers since 1848. They traveled in horse- or ox-drawn covered wagons along the route history would call "The Oregon Trail." They made this remarkable journey on an annual basis until the Civil War.

It was not an easy trek. Despite the camaraderie of campfire sing-alongs and the excitement of new experiences, they faced the hazards of cholera, influenza, dysentery, snake bites, Indians, and accidents. The weather sometimes added unwelcome elements of misery.

Harrison Kincaid, editor of Lane County's prestigious paper, the *Oregon State Journal*, made the journey with his parents in 1851 when he was 17 years old. He recalled the problems in a memoir:

"In Nebraska we encountered continuous rain, and sometimes the water level was up to the level of the wagon bed. After several weeks and 300 miles of steady rain, our clothes were wet through. With no way to get them dry, we often slept in wet clothes. After it stopped raining, we drove through miles of land so dry that our damp clothes were covered with a layer of dust."

It should come as no surprise that when these pioneers arrived in Lane County they felt they'd arrived in a Garden of Eden. Cabins went up, later houses. Communities soon formed.

Churches arrived soon after a community began. The first church in the county emerged from the meetings of seven Baptists on Mahlon Harlow's property, west of present Armitage Park, called "The Forks." Other denominations soon followed. The region's few roads were mostly ruts and mud, so settlers formed their towns near rivers, which could be navigated by canoe, raft, and later the bustling steamboat. They learned to choose their townsites with care. Eugene Skinner first platted his town too close to the Willamette River. The flooding water promptly washed it away, and local citizens dubbed it "Skinner's Mudhole." A major replatting moved the town farther from the river. Even so, floods occurred frequently for another century until flood control dams were built upstream on the

Willamette and its tributaries starting in the 1950s.

But the river brought gifts as well as trouble. In 1851 or '52 a civic leader named Hilyard Shaw dug out an old slough and diverted Willamette water into a millrace to power new industry, starting with a sawmill and a grist mill. Nearby Springfield finished a similar millrace in 1854 to begin another industrial complex that produced lumber and flour.

Five years later, in 1859, Oregon became a state. John Whiteaker, a Lane County pioneer, became its first governor. Whiteaker promoted many changes beneficial to the new state such as less waste in public business and better treatment of the "insane and idiotic." He also moved the penitentiary from Portland to Salem, the state capital.

He actively supported slavery, however. He gained a certain notoriety for such pro-slavery statements as "Abolition ought to be abolished," and "The south can never be conquered." Some politicians responded with fury, a feeling echoed by editor William Adams writing in his *Oregon Argus*. Whiteaker, he said, was at heart "as rotten a traitor as Jefferson Davis." But Judge Matthew Deady of Eugene argued that "'Old Whit,' although wrong in the head in politics, is honest and right in the heart."

After his term ended in 1862, Whiteaker lived in Pleasant Hill until his death in 1904. He lies in Eugene's Masonic Cemetery under a tombstone resembling a Conestoga covered wagon.

The year of statehood was also the year of Lane County's first fair. Henry Cummins, one of the county's resident intellectuals of the era, kept a lively diary and frequently passed judgment on daily events.

"Attended the agriculture fair of this county," he wrote. "Some excellent things exhibited." He recorded that $80.75 had been awarded in prize money for such categories as butter, fruit, cheese, and horses and that Governor Whiteaker enhanced the occasion with a fine speech. "Lane County done good for the first time," concluded Henry Cummins.

Not all residents had Henry's intellectual acumen, but it wasn't long before thoughts turned to education beyond high school. In 1856 Cumberland Presbyterians started Columbia College in Eugene City. It was more or less in operation until 1860 when its doors closed due to financial problems and dissension among its board members who argued bitterly over slavery issues. Sixteen years would elapse until the University of Oregon opened in 1876.

John Whiteaker, first governor of Oregon, about 1860.

One of Columbia College's more flamboyant students was Joaquin Miller, who later gained worldwide acclaim as the "Poet of the Sierras." Miller arrived in Lane County in 1853 with his parents on their donation land claim near Coburg. In 1860 he edited the *Democratic Register*. A southern sympathizer, Miller expressed fiery views in his paper. He called President Lincoln "a narrow-minded pedagogue," and he attacked the Civil War, remarking "there will be no cotton because there will be no nigger to produce it." County Republicans cried "treason," and the paper succumbed to political and economic pressures after three months. Miller marched on to fame on the lecture circuit.

Joaquin Miller, famed "Poet of the Sierras," about 1870.

Joaquin's brother George proved equally entertaining to early residents. George loved the seaport village of Florence on the

Oregon coast. He platted Florence's Chicago Addition in 1887. He expressed delight when George H. Colter founded the community of Glenada right across the Siuslaw River, believing the two cities would not compete but would help each other grow.

George Miller thought everyone should visit Florence, and he proposed an intercontinental road connecting the west coast to New York. He called it "the Florence/New York Super Highway." In 1933 the U. S. government adapted one of Miller's maps showing a highway leading from New York west straight to Ontario, Oregon, and then over the McKenzie Pass and on to Florence.

As a young man George often watched the birds on his father's farm. "I considered that if a goose could fly, so could a man," he said. Fifteen years later he built this model for a flying machine to be eight feet high and sixteen feet across. Its two sets of wings were made of bamboo and silk mounted on hollow shafts. They turned in opposite directions when the pilot pedaled with both feet and hands. He patented the device in 1892, eleven years before the Wright brothers flew theirs at Kitty Hawk. Among critics of the idea was George's brother, Joaquin. "Let the flying machine alone," he advised. "It's unnatural to fly, therefore it will not do. It is only a damn craze."

Whatever its failures as a western highway terminus, Florence did gain federal attention as a seaport. In 1890 Congress appropriated $50,000 for a jetty at the mouth of the Siuslaw River. But Captain Thomas Symonds of the U. S. Engineers said the river was not worth improving. That so angered the citizens of Florence that they hanged Symonds in effigy. Later Symonds revised his figures. Work on the jetty led to Florence becoming an important fishing and lumber port despite its remote location away from the county's population center in the southern Willamette Valley.

Meanwhile, settlement in the eastern region of the county increased. As immigrants scooped up the prime home sites on the valley floor, later arrivals moved farther afield, carving out a living on farms and ranches around Oakridge, Lowell, Winberry Creek, Cottage Grove, and Creswell. They soon learned to take advantage of the county's natural resources. Logging became a major industry of the upper Willamette and McKenzie regions when railroads were built after the turn of the century. Logging and lumbering brought new sawmills and new vitality to small upriver communities.

By 1870 river logging had become the primary means of getting logs from the woods to the sawmills. Horses or oxen hauled the logs to the river shore where they were stockpiled until spring when mountain

George Melvin Miller

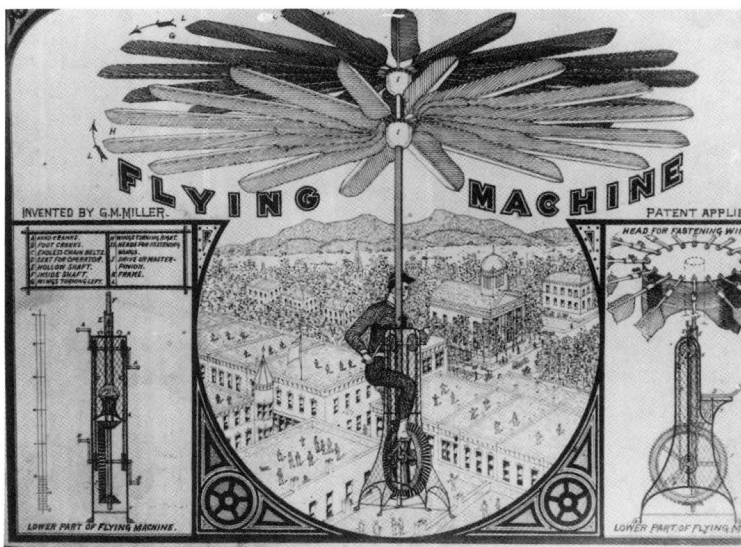

George Miller's magic flying machine.

snows melted and combined with spring rains to raise the level of the rivers. Logs were then floated down the McKenzie and Willamette to mills in Springfield, Eugene, and Coburg, and down the Mohawk to Wendling, Marcola, and Mabel.

By 1910 most river logging had ended, replaced by horses dragging logs to a skid road or to a logging railroad. When steam donkey engines came into use, they dragged logs to a waiting Shay locomotive, and the day's output was hauled to a nearby mill. Donkeys often proved dangerous, too, as they had a tendency to explode if the pressure rose too high.

Gold became another natural resource to be exploited. Its discovery in 1863 in the Blue River area caused a genuine outbreak of gold fever. But many claims produced mostly sore backs and broken dreams. A few mines produced quite well, such as the Lucky Boy, discovered in 1887 and potentially productive even to this day on a limited scale.

The Bohemia mines above Cottage Grove, discovered in 1863, provided a major economic boost to that area. Most of these mines have been prospected out, but under the aegis of the Bohemia Mine Owners Association, two of the deep mines have continued to operate.

Instead of gold, the Black Butte mountains near Cottage Grove produced cinnabar, a heavy, bright red mineral, the principal ore of mercury. Discovered in the 1890s the Black Butte mine operated off and on until 1969.

Probing for gold and timber deep into the forests created a need for bridges across the many rivers and streams. Most of the covered bridges were built by a contractor named Nels Roney who painted them red and signed them with his name and the date. Unfortunately, none of Roney's bridges have survived, although 19 other covered bridges have been preserved in the county.

Cal Young, about 1934.

Continuing to utilize the county's natural resources, residents turned hot springs into popular recreation sites, notably Belknap and Foley on the McKenzie River and McCredie southeast of Oakridge. In 1904 Levi Geer turned a hop house into a spacious hotel near the mineral waters of Calapooya Springs at London, south of Cottage Grove. The resort became so popular that Geer added a race track with grandstands and horses for hire— also a park with croquet and swings and a bathhouse for soaking in the mineral water piped from the springs.

In 1909 he bottled the mineral water, calling it "Cal-A-Poo-Ya Smiling Water." He planned to distribute it throughout the country. His plan quickly failed, however, mainly due to the invention of artificial carbonation. The resort fell into disuse, the springs dried up, and London became a small, peaceful country community.

But recreation takes many forms, and no discussion of Lane County would be complete without mentioning one of its most prominent citizens, Cal Young, chiefly remembered as one of the main organizers of the Oregon Trail Pageant. Originally known as the "Trail to Rail," the pageant began in 1926 to commemorate the completion of the Natron railroad cutoff, a faster link to California by way of the Willamette Pass.

Held every three years (with exceptions such as during World War II), the pageant featured two parades and a king and queen. Men were required to grow a beard and women wore long skirts. In the evening festive performances played out a recurring theme: the origin and growth of Oregon. In their book, *The Story of Eugene*, the Wilkins sisters said, "The cast would include some 2,500 people; their services would be voluntary, and the entire project would be dyed-in-the-wool, homespun, colossal, amateur to the last word."

But as the pageant's popularity increased, it lost its "homespun" quality and resembled a Hollywood extravaganza with professional actors. It became expensive and the last pageant was held in 1950.

The more adventurous pioneers could not resist exploring their beautiful countryside, pushing more and more into the nether regions. To the east the Three Sisters captivated many of them. Early settlers knew the three mountains as Faith, Hope, and Charity. The date of the first climb is obscure, perhaps 1874. George Collier, professor at the newly established University of Oregon, climbed them in 1880. Collier Glacier, the largest glacier in the Three Sisters area, bears his name.

In 1884 Thomas C. Judkins and John Eakins were the first to bivouac overnight on top of one of the mountains. The solitude, the breathtaking beauty of the scene atop the 10,047-foot Middle Sister made a lasting impression on Judkins. Years later, writing about his travels, he commented, "I think that never have my spirits soared so high as they did through the different hours of that long night on an Oregon mountain."

They didn't need to climb mountains to enjoy the McKenzie River. Fishing a river with as many rapids and eddies as this required a knowledgeable guide. The most famous McKenzie River guide was Prince Helfrich, who began guiding hunters and fishermen in the McKenzie River area in 1920. He organized the McKenzie River Guides Association in 1931, and in 1937 the guides began an annual float down the river a week before fishing season opened to check changes in the river's course and locate fishing spots. For 20 years they enjoyed a

leisurely day on the river, accompanied by their wives and a picnic lunch.

Around 1957 others began to join them. People floated down the river in everything from canoes and rubber rafts to homemade boats and inner tubes. A few rode in the McKenzie River driftboats, locally designed and built especially for the McKenzie River.

The event attracted spectators who eventually numbered in the thousands lining the banks. Thus began the annual White Water Parade, one of the Northwest's most unusual water parades. But the guides became increasingly worried that someone would drown. Riverside property owners began complaining about trespassers, strewn litter, and damaged property. The guides ended the parade in 1970 after two deaths by drowning occurred.

Early recreational outings entailed inordinate amounts of time and discomfort, especially when traveling by horse and buggy. A trip by stagecoach to the hot springs up the McKenzie River required fresh horses at Walterville, Vida, and Blue River. With luck, the lunch stop was at Leaburg. Four to eight people could be seated in the stages, which had no overhead cover. Passengers often arrived at their destination hot, wet, or muddy.

Going by stagecoach to the coast at Florence also was an exercise in grit and determination. Passengers planned on a bone-jolting ride of at least 14 hours. They traveled by stage 23 miles west to Hale Valley, then switched to a low, open buckboard wagon which wouldn't easily tip over on tortuous mountain roads. Three miles from Mapleton weary passengers got out and walked the remaining distance to the community where they could take a boat downstream on the Siuslaw River to Florence. Meanwhile the buckboard, unable to negotiate the three-mile footpath, took a winding 13 miles to reach the same destination.

One of the most famous stagecoach drivers was Ed McClanahan who drove the stage 57 miles between Eugene and Oakland, Oregon, carrying gold as well as passengers. His round trip took two days.

McClanahan, a big man with a flowing white beard and rosy cheeks, resembled an oversized leprechaun. His nickname was Lord Chesterfield because of his dapper white shirt, vest, and tie. Besides driving a stagecoach, he had a national reputation in the poultry industry for inventing a new type of chicken incubator, manufactured in a shed on his Millrace property. He lived there for 60 years, renting a fleet of canoes when the Millrace became an important recreational site.

Slowly transportation in the county improved. The first train arrived in Eugene in 1871. In 1911 a fancy station rose to accommodate the electric train line from Portland. Typical of that era, depots were surrounded by a lovely formal park—to impress passengers on the train with local charm and beauty.

Trolleys soon appeared on city streets. In Eugene the first system, begun in 1891, was a mule-drawn trolley driven by a black man named Wiley Griffin. It ran from the Southern Pacific depot to the University of Oregon. When Wiley got to campus and found no one waiting for a return trip, he tied the mule to a tree and browsed through the University's newly built Villard Hall. He often found his trolley full of impatient riders when he returned.

The automobile slowly gained popularity, although a number of folks grew apprehensive about a contraption that zipped along at a life-threatening 20 to 30 miles an hour.

In 1911 the first streetcar line came to Springfield. Banner-waving Springfield citizens lined the streets to witness the first arrival over the new rail bridge. A streetcar official, A. C. Woodward, proclaimed that the line "makes one city out of Eugene and Springfield. We would like to see Springfield become as large as New York and Eugene as large as London."

That was the year Springfield voted to go "wet" while Eugene was "dry," so thirsty Eugeneans headed for Springfield saloons. When the saloons closed on Saturday night, two streetcars were hooked together to take the Eugene celebrants home. These cars gained the nickname "drunken special," and featured a sheriff's deputy riding along to protect the ladies and keep the drunks from fighting.

The first airplane landed in Eugene in 1918. Eugene native Ethan Newman recalled the plane landed in Conger's sheep pasture on West 11th. Schools were let out for the occasion, and the National Guard arrived to handle the crowd. In 1919 Oregon's first municipal airport was established on Chambers Street in west Eugene.

As the 1920s merged into the 1930s, economic activity had gained such momentum that few county residents realized they were heading into the depression. Major improvements in the municipal airport were completed in 1930. Reconstruction of the McKenzie Highway kept 1,800 people employed. Construction crews worked on the University of Oregon Art Museum until its completion in 1932.

But gradually area mills slowed down. The Matlock Mill in Veneta closed for two months. Booth-Kelly operated only part time. Railroads, relying on timber products, felt the drop in production.

Private and federal relief swung into action. Road work as relief continued, and the Lane County portion of the Coast Highway was finished in 1932.

A few isolated sawmills kept working, such as Pennington Lumber Company between Noti and Walton, which ran until 1937. With houses, a school, and stores close to the mill, these small lumber camps enabled families to stay together during the turmoil of the depression.

The economy improved in 1938-1939. WPA and PWA funded construction projects such as a new federal building. Rosboro Lumber Company located a new mill in Springfield. But World War II loomed on the horizon.

Lane County was much like the rest of the country during the war. Victory gardens. Ration stamps. No nylons. Blackouts and air raid tests. Posters proclaiming that "loose lips sink ships," and "Uncle Sam Wants You." Songs of hope: *When the Lights Go On Again All Over the World* and *I'll Be Seeing You.*

The county's landscape has changed since then. Agriculture remains important, but gone are the vast fields of hops and pole beans. Berries, filberts, peppermint, and bush beans continue. Sheep and cattle graze the lands around such rural communities as Lorane, Crow, Cottage Grove, Veneta, and Creswell. Wine production has emerged to a level of importance. Grass seed produced in Lane County grows lawns throughout the nation.

Environmental concerns and dwindling supplies of easily harvested timber have decreased timber production. Former logging towns such as Mapleton and Oakridge look to tourism as increasingly important.

But the trail to Oregon remains well traveled. Modern-day settlers come to Lane County largely for the same reason as their predecessors—the desire for a better life. They search out the snow-capped mountains where skiing and mountain climbing offer year-round recreation. They explore sparkling lakes, rivers, and forests, which provide opportunity for boating, fishing, and hiking.

In spite of an altered landscape, an ever-increasing population, and some loss of pristine lands, the beauty and mystery of Lane County continue to cast a spell. Old-timers and newcomers alike still regard it as an adventure in the Garden of Eden.
—LUCILE MCKENZIE ◆

CHAPTER TEN

Further Glimpses of History

1579. In June 1579 the English explorer Francis Drake guided his vessel, the *Golden Hind,* northward along the west coast of North America. At 42 degrees north latitude—destined centuries later to mark the border between California and Oregon—the weather promptly turned bad. As a crew member recorded at the time (spelling modernized):

". . . We came into 42 deg. of North latitude, where in the night following we found such alteration of heat, into extreme and nipping cold, that our men in general did grievously complain thereof, some of them feeling their healths much impaired thereby. . . ."

But the stalwart crew continued two degrees farther north, which brought them off the coast of what would one day become Lane County, Oregon.

At that point the complaints bordered on insurrection, according to the writer, a minister and adventurer named Francis Fletcher: "The heat of the sun prevails not."

". . . Our meat, as soon as it was removed from the fire, would presently be frozen up, and our ropes and tackling in a few days were grown to that stiffness, that what 3 men before were able with them to perform, now 6 men, with their best strength and uttermost endeavor, were hardly able to accomplish: whereby a sudden and great discouragement seized upon the minds of our men. . . ." (Smith, 1979.)

Thus was logged one of the earliest complaints about the climate at 44 degrees north latitude. This and similar complaints about the region Captain (later "Sir Francis") Drake named New Albion would discourage further exploration of the Pacific Northwest coast for two centuries.

1778. Two centuries after Drake's adventure, Captain James Cook sailed from Hawaii toward the coast of New Albion in March in delightfully balmy weather. How was it, he wondered, that Captain Drake should have run into such dreadful weather in the month of June? But on his approach to the "long looked-for coast of New Albion," Cook himself ran into weather so bad that he named a headland (located to the north of the present Lane County coast) "Cape Foul Weather." The name stands to this day.

1850s. A place called Woodyville—or more informally, Woody's Landing—grew up during this decade on the banks of the Willamette River, about two and a half miles north of present-day Junction City. It later became known as Lancaster. It was a rough-and-tumble kind of place, complete with saloon and river dock, sometimes called "the fightin'est town on the river." Soon a scattering of homes and businesses joined the community, including the biggest of them all, Hand & Campbell, which advertised itself as the "Empire Store! Pre-Eminent." With cavalier spirit, the community proclaimed itself the head of navigation on the Willamette River, which it often was during low-water periods when the river boats could not push their way upstream through the shallows to Eugene City.

But the Willamette, like many great rivers, had a habit of meandering through its wide valley. That's what happened in the great flood of 1861—a devastating event for the entire valley that involved great loss of property and livestock. During that high water, the river changed course, cut a new channel to the east, and one day Woodyville/Lancaster awoke to find that it was no longer a river port. The Willamette's new course lay almost a mile to the east. (Corning, p. 158-164.)

1860s. Henry Clay Huston was one of the intellectuals of Lane County during this decade—from various accounts a highly principled man who served briefly in the Oregon Legislature (but resigned because he found politics too corrupt). He variously served as farmer, school teacher, volunteer soldier, journalist, and paralegal authority in demand for drawing up deeds, wills, and court papers. In 1852 he established a land claim west of Eugene and began a journal. The journal complains frequently of bad weather, but occasionally it blossoms into keen personal insights into the life of a bachelor farmer in the 1860s:

Sunday April 16, 1865. Started to Eugene City and heard Lincoln was killed. Day cloudy with little rain!

Monday 17. Showery and cool for the season of the year! In Eugene City: great excitement over the assassination of Lincoln. Abolitionists talking blood and thunder. Review threatened. Democrats are held responsible for the act of Booth.

Tuesday 18. Considerable rain last night. In Eugene again! Excitement still intense, talk of riots and mobs. . . . Pengra [pro-Lincoln editor] cooled down! Democrats determined and cool. News came that mobs were numerous through the country! Oregonian talks death without mercy, to Democrats. . . .

Sunday 23. A pleasant day, cool and hazy. . . . Disgusted with the human race and re-solved to turn my back on womenkind; for these reasons—Either I am a fool or they are fools. What I admire they do not; honesty is a trait not developed till after the honeymoon. To please a woman is to be a slave, to be independent is an insult, to win we must lie, to please we must deceive. And as I cannot stoop to lie, I of course must be discarded by all sensible females. Deception I hate, therefore I am and have been doomed to live and pine alone, and may die so!

Wednesday, May 10. . . . Today I complete my 37th year, poor, miserable, and lonesome, lost when in company most; neglected by the world generally, subjected to ingratitude and actually reduced to want while hundreds of dollars are due me for time, labor, and property once my own. . . . As admirer of virtue and chastity among women; a lover of beauty and charmed with wit of women, I desired the comforts of social happiness and imagined that some day I might enjoy wedded bliss with some refined female; but poverty has barred the pleasure of female society, and living a contemptible bachelor is the reward of my respect for the other sex. . . .

Saturday, May 5, 1866. A clear, warm, sunny day. At Isaac Zumwalt's—made a matrimonial proposition and left it under consideration. (Huston, 1968.)

Editor's Note: Lydia Ann Zumwalt, daughter of Isaac Zumwalt, accepted Mr. Huston's "matrimonial proposition," and they were married two months later. Born in Indiana in 1828, Huston died in 1899.

1870s. The barkentine sailing ship *Florence* was built in Bath, Maine, in 1840. She carried rum, molasses, and cotton along the east coast, then joined the burgeoning lumber trade on the west coast in the early 1860s. In 1875, enroute from Puget Sound to San Francisco, she ran into a gale 40 miles off the mouth of the Umpqua River. Eight men took to a lifeboat and rowed to within sight of the stormy coast with its deadly surf. The ship's captain, aboard the lifeboat, was wary of landing the tiny boat in the heavy surf but agreed to try when the others pleaded that it was their only chance of survival. The boat capsized and only one sailor, Daniel Dreary, lived to tell the tale and give a report of the tragedy to *The Oregonian* (November 25, 1875). Indians found him washed up on the beach, and they took him to the nearby community of Gardiner.

For weeks afterward, lumber and assorted debris washed up on nearby beaches. Among the flotsam was a white board bearing the name *Florence*. According to legend, the board was propped up against the Moody Store in the unnamed settlement by the Siuslaw River, and later it was nailed over the door of a new hotel, making it the Florence Hotel. (Lomax, 1968.)

It is true that the name Florence has stayed with the community since that time, though some doubt remains as to whether the town was named for the scrap of board washed up on the shore. More likely it was named for A. B. Florence, a state legislator from Lane County, according to Lewis L. McArthur's *Geographic Names*.

1880s. Fred Warner and his family lived on Fall Creek and enjoyed cordial relations with a group of Molalla Indians who camped summers in a wooded hollow near their home. Among them was a youngster of 12 named *Kwis-Kwis* ("Little Squirrel") whose parents had died. An aunt assumed his care but times were tough, and food was scarce. The aunt decided to sell Little Squirrel. She approached the Warner family, who, feeling sorry for the boy, agreed to take him in. Soon the deal was cast: Little Squirrel in exchange for two pumpkins and a pan of flour. He assumed a new name, Charley Tufti. The boy was shy but learned fast, learned English, even how to spell words. But when he

Charlie Tufti, right, with his adoptive brother, Frank S. Warner, about 1880.

showed his new knowledge to his Indian friends the next summer they scoffed and laughed and derided him. It is said that he never spoke English again, though he understood it perfectly.

Charley gained respect as a hard worker, especially during harvest season on various farms. He became a crack shot, and made money selling deer skins for glove making. A young woman named Sally, from the Klamath tribe, happened by one summer and captured the shy boy's heart. It appears they flirted with the eyes but few words emerged because she spoke no English and they didn't understand each other's dialect. But with a group of ladies present one evening after dinner he did manage to blurt out in Chinook jargon, *"Klahowya mika kloochman?"* And she understood. She replied, *"Klahowya mika man?"*

The white women present had just witnessed a proposal of marriage, and an acceptance—Indian style. (Translation: "How are you, my woman?" "How are you, my man?")

Charley became a local celebrity. He and his white brother, Frank Warner, are credited with the discovery and naming of a 286-foot waterfall southeast of Oakridge—Salt Creek Falls. Charley is credited with the discovery of Lane County's major lake, an incredibly pure lake at 5,412 feet elevation in the Cascade Mountains, variously called Virgin and Pengra Lake, but now known as Waldo Lake. Charley and another Indian named Chuck Chuck were able, with the aid of a white friend, to homestead 80 acres of their ancestral land east of Oakridge.

Tragically, Sally and their child died, probably from tuberculosis. Charley remarried but lost his second wife and two children, also to disease. He then married a Warm Springs Indian named Lucy. They had two children, Josephine, who graduated from Chemawa Indian School, and Jasper who ran the commissary at Warm Springs. Eventually they sold their holdings and retired to the Indian reservation. Charley died in 1908 in a logging accident. A peak six miles southeast of Oakridge, Tufti Mountain, 3,213 feet, was named in his honor. (Williams.)

1880s. Outdoor cooking was quite a challenge at isolated camps in the vast mountain wilderness of early Lane County. The most daring of camp cooks attempted to bake biscuits, no easy task under primitive conditions. Camp biscuits that did not turn out well promptly earned the name "deathballs." Sometime in the early years of this decade a surveying party camped in a locale near the juncture of the McKenzie River's South Fork with the main river. Members of the crew attempted to bake biscuits. The attempt was such a colossal failure that it caused the surveyors to honor the occasion with a permanent memorial. On their survey maps they designated a nearby promontory *Deathball Rock*. (McArthur, p. 242.)

1890s. The news from Deadwood Valley. In early times, Eugene newspapers maintained a set of country correspondents who provided information about their respective communities: marriages, births, deaths, cougar hunts, new settlers, the rutabaga harvest, and the removal of 150 head of cattle to Bald Mountain for summer grazing. The biggest news to come out of Deadwood Valley—a remote settlement in the coastal mountains east of Florence—was the report in the *Eugene City Guard* (April 4, 1894) from an unnamed gentleman correspondent reporting the regular meeting of the Woman's Union of Deadwood Valley. The meeting moved into executive session, and excluded the correspondent. At the close of the meeting, the resourceful reporter offered to buy a new dress for one of the ladies if she'd reveal what went on in the secret conclave. This is what she told him: A member asked for a re-reading of the following resolution which had been approved three years earlier:

"Resolved: that a three years limit of celibacy be placed on all bachelors, and those not married at the end of that time be run out of the settlement or hung."

Toward the end of the three-year grace period, most of the bachelors remained unmarried. They petitioned the ladies for a one-year extension of the deadline on the grounds of hard economic times.

A stormy debate ensued. The married women argued in favor of the extension; the single women opposed it. They argued that if times were hard, that's all the more reason the men should wed. The economies of togetherness meant that two could share the same house, warm themselves and cook by the same fire, sit at the same dinner table, even share the same bed.

Finally it came to a vote. All the married members voted in favor of the extension. All the single women voted against it. The extension was granted—simply because the Woman's Union included more married members than single. (*Lane County Historian*, Fall 1982, p. 54.)

1900s. The story of Opal Whiteley remains one of the great literary mysteries to come out of the backwoods of Oregon. At the age of six—that would put the year at 1903—Opal was said to have written a diary about her young life and her communion with nature in the woods around Cottage Grove. It was mostly a childish scrawl printed by crayon on paper bags and other scraps of paper. It was full of delightfully childish insight, and contained a kind of lyrical tone. She wrote thus of the harmonies of nature: "Earth-voices are glad voices, and earth-songs come up from the ground through the plants, and in their flowering, and in the days before these days are come, they do tell the earth-songs to the wind. And the wind in her goings does whisper them to folks to print for other folks, so other folks do have knowings of earth's songs. When I grow up, I am going to write for children—and grownups that haven't grown up too much—all the earth-songs I now do hear."

It was a literary sensation some 17 years later when *The Atlantic Monthly* magazine published it under the title, "The Story of Opal: Journal of an Understanding Heart." Remarkable that a child of six, daughter of an Oregon logger and his wife, could write such prose. Skeptics, who suggested she probably wrote it at the age of 20 shortly before publication, admitted nonetheless that the prose was colorful and weighty. "You can't

Lane County
Historian
The Lane County Historical Society
Vol. 41, No. 1   Spring 1996

"Fabulous Opal Whiteley" revisited

Opal Whiteley as "cover girl" in a 1996 issue of the *Lane County Historian.* (Photo: University of Oregon.)

read the diary without being enthralled," exclaimed a professor of literature. Some were even more skeptical of her subsequent claims to have been born of French royalty—kidnapped as an infant and exiled to a hopelessly remote locale in the woods of Oregon, where presumably she would never be heard from again. Remarkably, she was accepted by European royalty in subsequent travels to Europe and India. But in 1948 she was committed to a mental hospital in England where she died in 1992 at 94. Highgate Cemetery lists her under two names: Opal Whiteley and Françoise Marie de Bourbon-Orléans. (McQuiddy.)

1920s. The historical record gives mixed reports on Indians encountered by the pioneer settlers of Lane County. Many pioneer documents give reports of cordial relations along with occasional disputes. Legendary outdoor guide Prince Helfrich recalled the scenes of Indian seasonal migrations, and encampments, complete with tepees and fires, in Cascade mountain meadows in the summer. One time (late 1920s perhaps, or early '30s) he met an ancient Indian traveling with the summer migration. His companions said he had survived 107 summers. "That night I talked to the old man through an interpreter. . . . He told in detail of the great game trails where they would lie in wait for deer and elk and how the Indians would drive the game through a runway to other Indians who were waiting with bows and arrows. Brush would be burned in the fall as the Indians returned to Eastern Oregon. Since it was late in the season, the fall rains would soon extinguish the fires before any great damage was done. The burning made easier access through the country, as well as foraging for horses and big game animals." (Helfrich, p. 31.)

Miscellaneous. The most popular place name in Lane County appears to be "Cedar." The county has no fewer than 14 Cedar Creeks, along with a couple of Cedar Springs and one Cedar Swamp. Also within the county are nine Bear Creeks, nine Deer Creeks, nine Small Creeks, seven Alder Creeks, and seven Rock Creeks. However, there is only one Deadwood Creek, one Burp Hollow, and one Swastika Mountain. (*Atlas of Lane County*.)

Over the years, Lane County has had 178 post office names, though five of them never opened. The active ones included such exotic names as Mirth, Egypt, Paris, London, Rattlesnake, and Deadwood. Of those, only Deadwood remained in 1998, along with 22 others.—KEN METZLER

CHAPTER ELEVEN

Lane County Photographers
A Visual Memory

LANE COUNTY HAS BEEN SERVED since 1854 by many professional photographers—one count shows about 50 by 1920—and recorded by thousands of amateurs, some of them highly skilled. Over the years the stories, and often even the identities, of those who gave us this pictorial record have been lost or misplaced. Thus it is not unusual that fewer than half of the photographs printed here can be attributed to any particular photographer.

The first of Lane County's photo-historians was Philip F. Castleman, a miner ('49er) and entrepreneur. Early in the development of Eugene City he acquired photographic equipment and set up shop near what is now Willamette and Broadway to make daguerreotypes—the first commercially practical photographs, made on polished silvered surfaces and protected by small cases. Although no known examples of his early work survive, his photos were probably involved in the making of an 1859 lithographic print showing the budding town and its principal buildings.

In 1860 Castleman took on a partner, John A. Winter (1831-1916). Winter took over their studio on Willamette Street in 1862 and maintained the business, recording the growing town and its inhabitants for the rest of the century. His son, Clarence L. Winter (1865-1926), began making photographs in the early 1880s.

Winter had competition in the early years from (among others) Robert L. Forbes who maintained a studio in Eugene City from 1867 to 1876. Winter's studio was taken over (briefly in 1868 while Winter worked in Albany) by James G. Crawford. Various other photographers passed through, notably A. H. Wulzen who photographed a panorama of Eugene City about 1876, and Frank G. Abell, who passed through in 1877 and became a leader in the Portland portrait business in the 1880s. Part of Wulzen's panorama remains at the University of Oregon.

Until the early 1880s photography in Lane County attracted few amateurs, mainly because of the complexity of the chemical process and the need to have a darkroom laboratory close at hand. Around 1880 the development of ready-made dry-process glass plates made photography easier and much more accessible. Gelatin-based emulsions became faster, so the shutter came into use. Lane County still had only a few amateurs but more professionals arrived. Among them were A. L. Jackson and Frank A. Rankin. Another, John B. Rhinehart, was perhaps more noted in the community from his operation of a theater, new in 1884.

During the 1880s and 1890s the dry plate negative and improved transportation made it possible for photographers to wander the countryside with ease. They supplemented portrait work with landscapes and photos of farms, usually with tenants posed in front of them, horses and wagons and industrial scenes. In almost all of these the people were posed rather stiffly (everybody remembered the days when a headbrace was needed to prevent movement) and in plain view of the camera. If the photographer wanted to sell a copy to each subject, that person had to be easily visible. It was said

Eugene photographer Elizabeth Romane displays the day's catch, about 1918.

Chester Stevenson, early photographer, with his Graflex camera, about 1916.

that you weren't a logger until you had your picture taken cutting down a tree. The photo was delivered to the buyer mounted on a standard-sized piece of cardboard with the photographer's name imprinted.

George Eastman pretty much invented modern photography with the introduction of the Kodak camera in 1888. The slogan, "you press the button, we do the rest" said it all—you could be a photographer without also being a chemist. With these technical advances the number of photographers began to increase rapidly. Some photographers are virtually unknown except for their names, such as Warner and Randolph and H. R. Ross, who recorded scenes around Marcola.

Lane County had several prominent professional woman photographers. Sue Dorris began working at the Winter Photo Company about 1891, then opened her own studio in 1901 and ran it until about the end of World War I. From 1907 until 1912 Lulu Tollman and her husband John operated a studio. Dorris took on an assistant in 1909, Elizabeth Erdmann Romane (1890-1970), who opened a studio with her husband Harry in 1918. Elizabeth Romane was still making portraits in the 1950s, estimating in 1959 that she had done about 30,000 of them over the years.

Some of the best photographic records of Lane County came from postcard photographers. Prominent among them were Eugene Lavalleur of the Patton Post Card Company of Salem. From 1908 to the 1920s he took high-quality views of most of Oregon, including Lane County. His business was bought by Wesley Andrews of Baker who also produced many local-area postcards. Chester Stevenson also photographed Lane County scenes for postcards. The most prominent local postcard photographer was Dot Dotson. He began his photo finishing business in Eugene in the early 1930s, and he supplemented his income by traveling around Lane County to record scenes for postcards. Many of the best postcard images from the 1920s to the 1950s are his.

Other prominent studios include those of E. F. Martin, responsible for portraits and especially school group photos in the 1910s and 1920s, and the Kennell-Ellis Studio, begun in Eugene in 1923. Earl Kennell of Colfax, Washington, took Ernest Ellis of Eugene as his partner. Eventually Kennell and Ellis built a small empire of studios around the Northwest. Their current studio occupies a 1946 structure on Willamette Street listed as a City of Eugene historic landmark. E. L. Lewis ran the old Mill Studio in Springfield and was prominent in local photography from the 1940s to the 1960s.

Several amateur photographers have contributed heavily to this book. J. Merle

Nighswander took photos on glass negatives in Hadleyville, near Crow, and other areas of western Lane County from about 1905 to about 1925. Smith Mountjoy worked for 42 years in the Booth-Kelly Lumber Mill, but he's best known for his photos of the Lane County hop harvest and of disasters such as the county's frequent floods.

Exactly which old photos survive and which photographers are known (none are really well known) has depended on a multitude of historical accidents. Photographs and their negatives are fragile so far as their historical preservation is concerned. When first made they are ordinary; later they become just "old things." Only after passage of time do they become "historic." Even then, much effort must be expended to collect, identify, and preserve them.

Picture maker's self portrait. Photographer Smith Mountjoy, who took many of the photos appearing in this book, put himself in this photo of a Southern Pacific crew on a pump car. He's kneeling on the right, and is taking the photo by a cable attached to the camera: June 14, 1910. (Photo: Smith Mountjoy.)

We should be grateful to the photographers for making these records. We should be equally grateful to those who have collected and preserved the records, for this is our collective visual memory.
—ERIC GUSTAFSON

Bibliography

Andrews, Ralph W. *This Was Logging*. Superior, 1954.

Atlas of Lane County, Oregon. James E. Meacham, ed. 1990.

Atlas of Oregon. William G. Loy, et al. 1976.

Atlas of Oregon Lakes. Daniel M. Johnson, et al. 1985.

Balfour, Helen. "Memories." In Edwards, O'Hearn, and Hing, *Sawdust & Cider: A History of Lorane, Oregon and the Siuslaw Valley*. 1987, p. 153.

Barton, Lois. *Spencer Butte Pioneers*. 1982.

Beckham, Stephen Dow. *Applegate Trail: Impressions and Experiences of Emigrants and Other Travelers*. Applegate Trail Coalition, 1995.

Below, Carl. "History of the Eugene Fire Department." *Lane County Historian*, Winter 1975-76, p. 43.

Byers, Ron. "Remembering Wendling." *Lane County Historian*, Spring 1997, p. 14.

Carrothers, Beulah H. "Indian Lore." *Lane County Historian*, June 1959, p. 42.

Carson, Rachel L. *The Sea Around Us*. Oxford, 1951.

"Cornelius Hills Family, The." Private journal, ND.

Corning, Howard McKinley. *Willamette Landings*. Oregon Historical Society, 1973.

Edwards, Patricia, Nancy O'Hearn, and Marna Hing. *Sawdust & Cider: A History of Lorane, Oregon and the Siuslaw Valley*. 1987.

"Elnans of Deadwood, The." *Lane County Historian*, Summer 1982, p. 56.

Fortt, Inez, "From Sacramento to Portland in Seven Days." *Lane County Historian*, Spring 1971, p. 3.

Frankel, Martha. "303 Willamette Street: Eugene's Green House on the Hill." *Lane County Historian*, Spring 1989, p. 3.

Hebert, Mrs. Clarence. "Historical Background of Oakridge, Oregon." *Lane County Historian*, September 1960, p. 28.

Helfrich, Prince. *Tales of the Oregon Cascades*. 1990.

Henrickson, James E. *Joe Lane of Oregon: Machine Politics and the Sectional Crisis, 1849-1861*. Yale, 1967.

Hills, Lawrence D. *Tales from the Hills*. 1982.

Hulin, Gilbert. "Eugene's Trolley Car Era," *Lane County Historian*, Spring 1973, p. 3.

Hunter, Wally. *The Bohemia Story*. 1969.

Huntington, Hallie Hills. "Glimpses of History—a Hallie Huntington Sampler." *Lane County Historian*, Spring 1994.

_____. *All the Way West*. 1984.

_____. *Mountain Trails*. ND.

Huston, Henry Clay. "Journal of Henry Clay Huston, 1864-1866." *Lane County Historian*, Winter 1968, p. 83.

Inman, Leroy B. *Beautiful McKenzie*. 1996.

"Joaquin Miller: A Letter from Lane County." *Lane County Historian*, Fall 1989, p. 55.

Johnese, Susan. "The Mt. June Flume." *The Dexter News*, November 1981.

Keepers, Walt. "A Home Away from Home." *Lane County Historian*, Summer 1985, p. 23.

Kelly, Sister M. Margaret Jean. *The Career of Joseph Lane: Frontier Politician*. Catholic University, 1942.

Lomax, Alfred L. "A Ship's Nameplate Makes History." *Lane County Historian*, Summer 1968, p. 55.

_____. "Early Shipping Industry in the Lower Siuslaw Valley." *Lane County Historian*, Summer 1971, p. 32.

McArthur, Lewis L. *Oregon Geographic Names*. 6th ed. 1992.

McQuiddy, Steve. "A New-Found Interest in 'Fabulous Opal Whiteley.'" *Lane County Historian*, Spring 1996, p. 6.

Metzler, Roxie. "Driving Oregon's Pioneer Off-Road Logging Trucks." *Lane County Historian*, Spring 1992, p. 15.

Miller, Joaquin. "A Ride Through Oregon." *Overland Monthly*, April 1872.

Moore, Lucia Wilkins. "John Whiteaker, First Governor of Oregon." *Lane County Historian*, February 1959, p. 3.

Moore, Lucia, Nina McCornack, and Gladys McCready. *The Story of Eugene*. 1949.

Moore, Merle. "Letters from Bohemia." *Lane County Historian*, Summer 1981, p. 31.

Nedelman, Irene C. "Cheshire, Then and Now." *Lane County Historian*, Fall 1987, p. 45.

Newman, Doug. "Solo Adventures Atop Lane County's Fire Lookouts." *Lane County Historian*, Summer 1992, p. 36.

Nolan, Edward W. *Coburg Remembered*. 1982.

Oregon Blue Book. 1997-98.

Oregon's Highway Park System: 1921-1989. Oregon Parks and Recreation Department, 1992.

Polley, Louis E. *A History of the Mohawk Valley and Early Lumbering.* 1984.

Rakestraw, Lawrence and Mary. *History of the Willamette National Forest.* 1991.

Richardson, Geneva. "Blacksmithing Takes a Turn." In *Golden Was the Past,"* Writers Discussion Group, 1970, p. 166.

Rust, Elma. *The Pioneers of Lake Creek Valley.* 1984.

Season of Harvest: Recollections of Lane County. Youth and Senior Exchange Project, 1975.

Smith, Leslie C. *Francis Drake in the Winds of Oregon June, 1579.* 1979.

Smith, Willis. "The Willis Smith Story." *The Early Days of the West Lane Domain,* Vol. 3, 1977, p. 20.

Thoele, Michael. *Bohemia: The Lives and Times of an Oregon Timber Adventure.* Oregon Historical Society, 1998.

Thomas, Anne. "Early Years on the Farm." In *Golden Was the Past,* Writers Discussion Group, 1970, p. 45.

Thompson, Herbert C. "Going to Portland in a Woodburner." *Lane County Historian,* March 1960, p. 4.

Tweedell, Bob. *Millrace History.* N.D.

Velasco, Dorothy. *Lane County: An Illustrated History of the Emerald Empire.* 1985.

Waldo, John Breckenridge. *Diaries and Letters from the High Cascades of Oregon 1880-1907.* U.S. Forest Service, 1989.

Walling, A. G. *Illustrated History of Lane County Oregon.* 1884.

Weiss, Elaine. "Jobs and Change in the Timber Industry." *Lane County Historian,* Summer 1993, p. 53.

Wilde, Chris T. *Early Days of Junction City, Oregon.* 1978.

Wilkinson, Betty. "My Life On Indian Creek." *Lane County Historian,* Spring 1987.

Williams, Catherine D. "Charley Tufti." *Lane County Historian,* Fall 1988, p. 55.

Williams, Jerold. "Hot Springs in Lane County." *Lane County Historian,* Winter 1974, p. 51.

Writers Discussion Group. *Cottage Grove, Oregon: Golden Was the Past.* 1970.

Wyatt, Steve. "The Flax Industry of Lane County." *Lane County Historian,* Summer 1990, p. 27.

Young, Cal. "A Pioneer Family Comes to Lane County." *Lane County Historian,* June 1957.

Index

THE END. (For this auto the end came quickly in an encounter with a train near Jasper about 1930.)